Ninja Foodi Smart XL Grill Cookbook for Beginners 2021

300 Ultimate Ninja Foodi Smart XL Grill Recipes for Beginners and Advanced Users | Tasty Indoor Grilling and Air Frying

Debbie K. Eduard

Table of Contents

Introduction

Did you have a look at the new Ninja Foodi Smart indoor grill? This advanced multipurpose electric grill is making a major buzz around the world due to its super-smart cooking functions, its effective grilling system, and the XL capacity. Ninja has several other electric grills launched; what makes this one different is a large size, the grilling presets, combined with other cooking programs, and an onboard temperature probe. Well, there is a lot more to know about this Ninja masterpiece, and in this cookbook, you will get to find everything about the Ninja Smart XL grill along with the variety of meaty treats and delicious meals that you can cook in this appliance for you and your whole family. So, let's get started.

Chapter 1: Meet the Ninja Foodi Smart XL Indoor Grill

The advanced multifunctional 6 in one kitchen miracle Ninja Foodi Smart Grill has made grilling an effortless experience. Who knew indoor grilling would become so easy to go someday? But now Ninja Foodi has introduced its mule purpose grill appliance, which allows you to grill, bake, roast, the air crisp, broil and dehydrate different food items. The device is available in XL size, and its cooking pot can accommodate a 4-quart Air crisper basket.

Perks of having Ninja Smart Grill

Are you still looking for reasons to buy this XL-sized indoor grill? Well, look no further, as we are about to share some of the most highlighting features of this grill. Following are a few of the known benefits that an electric grill like that of Ninja Foodi Smart Grill guarantees to provide:

1. Temperature Probing

What I really liked about this grill is that it comes with a temperature probe that is fixed on one side of the appliance. You can easily pull out the probe drawer, insert the probe into the meat that needs to be cooked and connect it to the thermometer port given on the same side of the appliance. Continue cooking as per the instructions; the probe will beep once the internal temperature of the meat reaches the desired point. This makes it super convenient, and you don't need to keep checking on the food all the time.

2. XL Capacity

The size matters when it comes to indoor grills. I always find it annoying when the electric grills do not provide enough space to cook a meal for the whole family. But with this XL sized electric grill, that is not a problem. It has a rectangular shape which can easily accommodate five full-size chicken legs, or a rib rack, and four pork chops at one time. To be honest, it was the size of this grill that first attracted me, and when I discovered all its smart cooking functions, I knew I wanted to have it.

3. Presets and Manual

The Ninja smart grill does not only come with six smart cooking programs, but it also provides different presets for grilling. When you select the grill function, you can either select the time and temperature using the given presets like FISH, BEEF, POULTRY, etc. or you can change the settings using the manual option. In this way, a user gets complete freedom of cooking any type of meal while keeping the quality and texture of the food as desired.

4. Splatter Sheet

It is yet another feature that makes the smart ninja grill different from other electric grills. It comes with a splatter sheet that is fixed over the grilling fan present on the underside of the lid. This splatter sheet protects the heating element and does not allow the food and its splatter to get into the fan or stick to it. Easy use and easy cleaning!

5. Energy Efficient

Most people think that electric grills might add a lot to their electricity bills. But that's not the case with the Ninja smart grill. Though these grills are reliant on electricity, yet they are energy efficient in this regard. About 1760 watts per hour of electricity is used while using an electric grill like Ninja Foodi Smart Grill. Moreover, do you to its large size you won't have to grill or cook the food in batches, and a single session of cooking keeps your electricity consumption minimum

Unboxing the Grill

The Ninja Smart XL indoor grill makes cooking and grilling convenient due to its great built and all the accessories that come along with it. The grilling unit comes with a flip lid, the cooking pots, plates, baskets, and a probe. The vent is present on the backside of the cooking unit, so make sure to keep the unit on a countertop with no other object blocking its vent. When you unbox the Ninja Foodi Smart XL indoor grill, here are the things that you will find in there.

- Ninja® Foodi Smart XL Indoor Grill
- Grill grate
- Crisper basket
- Cooking pot

- Removable splatter shield
- Onboard thermometer storage
- Foodi Smart thermometer
- Double-sided cleaning brush

Control Panel

The control panel of the grill is present on the front bottom of the appliance. On this panel, there is a display screen on top which have "up and down" keys for cooking time and temperature on both sides. The display screen does not only show cooking time and temperature when selected; it also indicates the selected:

- Preset: Beef, chicken, fish, etc.
- Med, med-rare and rare
- Lo, med, hi, and max

Below the display, there are keys given to select the cooking program. There are six different cooking programs to choose from:

1. Air Crisp
2. Roast
3. Grill
4. Bake
5. Broil
6. Dehydrate

Besides these keys, you will also find keys that say "MANUAL" and "PRESET." The preset option can be used to choose the desired grilling presets: beef, poultry, fish, etc. Whereas you can always use the manual button to change the temperature and timer settings. The Ninja smart grill offers the following range of temperatures to cook and grill a different variety of meals.

LOW (400°F)

- Bacon
- Sausages
- Using thick BBQ sauce

MED (450°F)

- Frozen meats
- Marinated/sauced meats

HI (500°F)

- Chicken
- Burgers
- Hot dogs
- Meat
- kebabs

MAX (up to 510°F)

- Steaks
- Veggies
- Fruit
- Pizzas
- Fresh/ frozen seafood
- Veggie
- Kebabs

Chapter 2: How to Use: Step by Step Cooking Guide

The use of the Ninja Foodi Smart Grill gets easy if we divide the whole process into three basic steps: Assemble, Prepare, And Cook!'

Setting Up the Indoor Grill

- For every session of cooking, you will need to assemble the device accordingly. First, clean the exterior and interior of the device with a clean cloth.
- Now plug in the device and press the power button to switch on the device.
- Open the lid of the Ninja Foodi Smart Grill.
- Place the ceramic coated cooking pot inside the grill. This basket is removable and dishwasher safe.
- Now depending on the cooking mode: Select grill grate for grilling, air crisp basket for air crisp option, crisper plate for dehydrating and grilling grate for baking, broiling, and roasting, etc. and place them in the ceramic coated cooking pot of the grill.
- Now the device is ready assembled.

Grilling

- Switch on the grilling device by pressing the Power Button.
- For grilling, place the grilling grate inside the cooking pot.
- You will have to press the "GRILL" key to select this function.
- Now, if you want to select from the presets, then press the PRESET key and use the ARROW keys on its left to change the PRESET from BEEF, to FISH or to Others.
- Use the other set of ARROW keys to change from RARE, MED RARE, MED, MED WELL, WELL for steaks, and other similar recipes.
- If you are NOT using the preset option, then press the MANUAL key and then select the TIME and TEMPERATURE by using their respective keys.
- Now press PREHEAT to initiate preheating; the progress bar will indicate the preheating.
- Insert the probe into the food if desired, connect it to its respective pot.
- Add food to the pot when the display says "ADD FOOD." Then close the lid.
- Once the cooking is finished, the display will indicate the END sign and REMOVE FOOD sign.

- Remove the food, its thermometer, and then serve.

Cooking on other modes

- If you are not grilling, then using other cooking programs for cooking.
- For that, press any of the respective keys "AIR CRISP, BROIL, BAKE, ROAST, DEHYDRATE.
- Make sure to place the accessories according to the cooking function that you are using.
- Once the mode is selected, simply select the cooking temperature and time by using their arrow keys.
- Let the device preheat to reach the required temperature.
- When it says to ADD FOOD, place the food inside, then cover the lid.
- Use the START/PAUSE key to start and stop the cooking operation when desired.
- You can flip and toss the food during every cooking session then resume cooking.
- Once done, the appliance will beep and indicate to REMOVE FOOD.
- Remember that in a continuous session, the Ninja foodi might not take much time for preheating the second time as it would already be preheated from the first session.
- Remove the food and allow your grill to cool down before moving to the next step of cleaning the device.

Cleaning and Maintenance

All the accessories of the Ninja smart indoor grill are dishwasher safe, so you can wash them easily in the dishwasher. Avoid scratching the accessories as it may damage their ceramic coating.

1. After cooking, unplug the device and allow it to cool down first.
2. Leave the lid open when the device is cooling down.
3. Remove the inner grills or baskets and the cooking pot and remove if there are any solid food particles in it.
4. Now you can either dish wash them carefully or wash them with soapy water to remove the grease.
5. Allow all the accessories to dry before putting them back into place.

6. Use the brush given with the grill to scrap of all the grease. Avoid using other hard brushes to prevent any damage.
7. Clean the base unit from the inside and the outside using a lightly wet cloth.
8. Do not immerse or wash the base unit or the lid with water.

Troubleshooting

1. Use only grill grate or inner basket, one at a time.
2. To avoid troubleshooting, check if the cooking pot is not overly stuffed or loaded.
3. Keep the food only up to 2/3 of the cooking pot's height and avoid overstuffing.
4. Check if the lid is properly closed before start cooking.
5. If the device is physically damaged, do not continue cooking and instantly call for customer support.

Frequently asked questions

1. Which accessory can I use for cooking on air crisp mode?

There is a separate 4-quart air crisp basket that comes with this grill. Set this basket inside the ceramic cooking pot of the grill and then put food in this basket for cooking. Grease the basket with cooking spray if needed.

2. Can we cook liquid food in the Ninja smart grill's cooking pot?

The Ninja Foodi Smart Grill is only designed for grilling, air crispy, baking, broiling, dehydrating, and roasting purposes; cooking liquid food like stews, soups in its cooking pot is not appropriate.

3. Is preheating necessary in the Ninja smart grill?

Yes, if you want your perfect cooked and crispy, then preheating will make it possible. Without preheating, the selected cooking temperature and time will not provide the desired results.

Chapter 3: Breakfast Recipes

Cinnamon Buttered Toasts

Preparation Time: 10 minutes
Cooking Time: 5 minutes
Servings: 3
Ingredients:

- ¼ cup sugar
- ¾ teaspoon ground cinnamon
- ¾ teaspoon vanilla extract
- 1/8 teaspoons freshly ground black pepper
- ¼ cup salted butter, softened
- 6 whole-wheat bread slices

Method:
1. In a bowl, add the sugar, vanilla, cinnamon, black pepper and butter and mix until smooth.
2. Spread the butter mixture over each bread slice evenly.
3. Arrange the "Crisper Basket" in the pot of Ninja Air Smart XL Indoor Grill.
4. Close the Ninja Air Smart XL Indoor Grill with lid and select "Air Crisp".
5. Set the temperature to 400 degrees F to preheat.
6. Press "Start/Stop" to begin preheating.
7. When the display shows "Add Food" open the lid and place the bread slices into the "Crisper Basket".
8. Close the Ninja Air Smart XL Indoor Grill with lid and set the time for 5 minutes.
9. Press "Start/Stop" to begin cooking.
10. When the cooking time is completed, press "Start/Stop" to stop cooking.
11. Open the lid and transfer the bread slices onto serving plates.
12. Cut the bread slice diagonally and serve.

Nutritional Information per Serving:

- Calories 341
- Total Fat 17.2 g
- Saturated Fat 10.1 g
- Cholesterol 41 mg
- Sodium 374 mg
- Total Carbs 40.5 g
- Fiber 4.1 g
- Sugar 19.9 g
- Protein 7.4 g

Eggs in Avocado Halves

Preparation Time: 10 minutes
Cooking Time: 12 minutes
Servings: 2
Ingredients:

- 1 avocado, halved and pitted
- Salt and ground black pepper, as required
- 2 eggs
- 1 tablespoon Parmesan cheese, shredded

Method:

1. Arrange a greased square piece of foil in the "Crisper Basket" in the pot of Ninja Air Smart XL Indoor Grill.
2. Close the Ninja Air Smart XL Indoor Grill with lid and select "Bake".
3. Set the temperature to 390 degrees F to preheat.
4. Press "Start/Stop" to begin preheating.
5. Carefully, scoop out about 2 teaspoons of flesh from each avocado half.
6. Crack 1 egg in each avocado half and sprinkle with salt, black pepper and cheese.
7. When the display shows "Add Food" open the lid and place the avocado halves into the "Crisper Basket".
8. Close the Ninja Air Smart XL Indoor Grill with lid and set the time for 12 minutes.
9. Press "Start/Stop" to begin cooking.
10. When the cooking time is completed, press "Start/Stop" to stop cooking.
11. Open the lid and transfer the avocado halves onto serving plates.
12. Top with Parmesan and serve.

Nutritional Information per Serving:

- Calories 278
- Total Fat 24.7 g
- Saturated Fat 5.9 g
- Cholesterol 165 mg
- Sodium 188 mg
- Total Carbs 9.1 g
- Fiber 6.7 g
- Sugar 0.8 g
- Protein 8.4 g

Scallion & Jalapeño Soufflé

Preparation Time: 10 minutes
Cooking Time: 8 minutes
Servings: 2
Ingredients:

- 2 tablespoons light cream
- 2 large eggs
- 1 tablespoon fresh scallion, chopped
- 1 jalapeño pepper, chopped
- Salt, as required

Method:

1. Arrange the "Crisper Basket" in the pot of Ninja Air Smart XL Indoor Grill.
2. Close the Ninja Air Smart XL Indoor Grill with lid and select "Air Crisp".
3. Set the temperature to 390 degrees F to preheat.
4. Press "Start/Stop" to begin preheating.
5. Grease 2 soufflé dishes.
6. In a bowl, add all ingredients and beat until well combined.
7. Divide the mixture into the prepared soufflé dishes evenly.
8. When the display shows "Add Food" open the lid and place the soufflé dishes into the "Crisper Basket".
9. Close the Ninja Air Smart XL Indoor Grill with lid and set the time for 8 minutes.
10. Press "Start/Stop" to begin cooking.
11. When the cooking time is completed, press "Start/Stop" to stop cooking.
12. Open the lid and serve hot.

Nutritional Information per Serving:

- Calories 82
- Total Fat 5.7 g
- Saturated Fat 2 g
- Cholesterol 188 mg
- Sodium 153 mg
- Total Carbs 1.3 g
- Fiber 0.3 g
- Sugar 0.9 g
- Protein 6.5 g

Bacon & Bread Cups

Preparation Time: 10 minutes
Cooking Time: 10 minutes

Servings: 2

Ingredients:

- 2 bread slices
- 1 bacon slice, chopped
- 4 tomato slices
- 1 tablespoon Mozzarella cheese, shredded
- 2 eggs
- 1/8 teaspoon maple syrup
- 1/8 teaspoon balsamic vinegar
- ¼ teaspoon fresh parsley, chopped
- Salt and ground black pepper, as required
- 2 tablespoons mayonnaise

Method:

1. Lightly, grease 2 ramekins.
2. Line each prepared ramekin with 1 bread slice.
3. Divide the bacon and tomato slices over bread slice in each ramekin.
4. Top with the cheese evenly.
5. Crack 1 egg in each ramekin over cheese.
6. Drizzle with maple syrup and vinegar and then sprinkle with parsley, salt and black pepper.
7. Arrange the "Crisper Basket" in the pot of Ninja Air Smart XL Indoor Grill.
8. Close the Ninja Air Smart XL Indoor Grill with lid and select "Air Crisp".
9. Set the temperature to 320 degrees F to preheat.
10. Press "Start/Stop" to begin preheating.
11. When the display shows "Add Food" open the lid and place the ramekins into the "Crisper Basket".
12. Close the Ninja Air Smart XL Indoor Grill with lid and set the time for 10 minutes.
13. Press "Start/Stop" to begin cooking.
14. When the cooking time is completed, press "Start/Stop" to stop cooking.
15. Open the lid and
16. Remove the ramekins and top each with mayonnaise.
17. Serve warm.

Nutritional Information per Serving:

- Calories 269
- Total Fat 18.2 g
- Saturated Fat 5.6 g
- Cholesterol 191 mg
- Sodium 224 mg
- Total Carbs 10.6 g
- Fiber 0.6 g
- Sugar 2.7 g

- Protein 16 g

Ham & Egg Bites

Preparation Time: 10 minutes
Cooking Time: 18 minutes
Servings: 6
Ingredients:

- 6 ham slices
- 6 eggs
- 6 tablespoons cream
- 3 tablespoon mozzarella cheese, shredded
- ¼ teaspoon dried basil, crushed

Method:

1. Arrange the "Crisper Basket" in the pot of Ninja Air Smart XL Indoor Grill.
2. Close the Ninja Air Smart XL Indoor Grill with lid and select "Bake".
3. Set the temperature to 350 degrees F to preheat.
4. Press "Start/Stop" to begin preheating.
5. Lightly grease 6 cups of a silicone muffin tin.
6. Line each prepared muffin cup with 1 ham slice.
7. Crack 1 egg into each muffin cup and top with cream.
8. Sprinkle with cheese and basil.
9. When the display shows "Add Food" open the lid and place the muffin cups into the "Crisper Basket".
10. Close the Ninja Air Smart XL Indoor Grill with lid and set the time for 18 minutes.
11. Press "Start/Stop" to begin cooking.
12. When the cooking time is completed, press "Start/Stop" to stop cooking.
13. Open the lid and serve warm.

Nutritional Information per Serving:

- Calories 202
- Total Fat 12.4 g
- Saturated Fat 4.9 g
- Cholesterol 205 mg
- Sodium 881 mg
- Total Carbs 3.4 g
- Fiber 0.7 g
- Sugar 0.6 g
- Protein 18.9 g

Spinach & Turkey Bites

Preparation Time: 15 minutes
Cooking Time: 23 minutes
Servings: 4
Ingredients:

- 1 tablespoon unsalted butter
- 1 pound fresh baby spinach
- 4 eggs
- 7 ounces cooked turkey, chopped
- 4 teaspoons unsweetened almond milk
- Salt and ground black pepper, as required

Method:

1. In a frying pan, melt the butter over medium heat and cook the spinach for about 2-3 minutes or until just wilted.
2. Remove from the heat and drain the liquid completely.
3. Transfer the spinach into a bowl and set aside to cool slightly.
4. Arrange the "Crisper Basket" in the pot of Ninja Air Smart XL Indoor Grill.
5. Close the Ninja Air Smart XL Indoor Grill with lid and select "Air Crisp".
6. Set the temperature to 355 degrees F to preheat.
7. Press "Start/Stop" to begin preheating.
8. Divide the spinach into 4 greased ramekins, followed by the turkey.
9. Crack 1 egg into each ramekin and drizzle with almond milk.
10. Sprinkle with salt and black pepper.
11. When the display shows "Add Food" open the lid and place the ramekins into the "Crisper Basket".
12. Close the Ninja Air Smart XL Indoor Grill with lid and set the time for 20 minutes.
13. Press "Start/Stop" to begin cooking.
14. When the cooking time is completed, press "Start/Stop" to stop cooking.
15. Open the lid and serve hot.

Nutritional Information per Serving:

- Calories 200
- Total Fat 10.2 g
- Saturated Fat 4.1 g
- Cholesterol 209mg
- Sodium 249 mg
- Total Carbs 4.5 g
- Fiber 2.5 g
- Sugar 0.8 g

- Protein 23.4 g

Cheddar & Cream Omelet

Preparation Time: 10 minutes
Cooking Time: 8 minutes
Servings: 2
Ingredients:

- 4 eggs
- ¼ cup cream
- Salt and ground black pepper, as required
- ¼ cup cheddar cheese, grated

Method:

1. Lightly, grease a 6x3-inch pan.
2. In a bowl, add the eggs, cream, salt, and black pepper and beat well.
3. Place the egg mixture into a greased 6x3-inch pan.
4. Arrange the "Crisper Basket" in the pot of Ninja Air Smart XL Indoor Grill.
5. Close the Ninja Air Smart XL Indoor Grill with lid and select "Air Crisp".
6. Set the temperature to 350 degrees F to preheat.
7. Press "Start/Stop" to begin preheating.
8. When the display shows "Add Food" open the lid and place the pan into the "Crisper Basket".
9. Close the Ninja Air Smart XL Indoor Grill with lid and set the time for 4 minutes.
10. Press "Start/Stop" to begin cooking.
11. After 4 minutes, sprinkle the omelet with cheese evenly.
12. Close the Ninja Air Smart XL Indoor Grill with lid and set the time for 4 minutes.
13. When the cooking time is completed, press "Start/Stop" to stop cooking.
14. Open the lid and serve hot.

Nutritional Information per Serving:

- Calories 202
- Total Fat 15.1 g
- Saturated Fat 6.8 g
- Cholesterol 348 mg
- Sodium 144 mg
- Total Carbs 1.8 g
- Fiber 0 g
- Sugar 1.4 g
- Protein 14.8 g

Mini Tomato Quiche

Preparation Time: 10 minutes
Cooking Time: 30 minutes
Servings: 2
Ingredients:

- 4 eggs
- ¼ cup onion, chopped
- ½ cup tomatoes, chopped
- ½ cup milk
- 1 cup Gouda cheese, shredded
- Salt, as required

Method:

1. In a large ramekin, add all the ingredients and mix well.
2. Arrange the "Crisper Basket" in the pot of Ninja Air Smart XL Indoor Grill.
3. Close the Ninja Air Smart XL Indoor Grill with lid and select "Air Crisp".
4. Set the temperature to 340 degrees F to preheat.
5. Press "Start/Stop" to begin preheating.
6. When the display shows "Add Food" open the lid and place the ramekin into the "Crisper Basket".
7. Close the Ninja Air Smart XL Indoor Grill with lid and set the time for 30 minutes.
8. Press "Start/Stop" to begin cooking.
9. When the cooking time is completed, press "Start/Stop" to stop cooking.
10. Open the lid and serve hot.

Nutritional Information per Serving:

- Calories 247
- Total Fat 16.1 g
- Saturated Fat 7.5 g
- Cholesterol 332 mg
- Sodium 417 mg
- Total Carbs 7.3 g
- Fiber 0.9 g
- Sugar 5.2 g
- Protein 18.6 g

Sausage & Scallion Frittata

Preparation Time: 15 minutes
Cooking Time: 20 minutes
Servings: 2

Ingredients:

- ¼ pound cooked breakfast sausage, crumbled
- ½ cup Cheddar cheese, shredded
- 4 eggs, beaten lightly
- 2 scallions, chopped
- Pinch of cayenne pepper

Method:

1. In a bowl, add the sausage, cheese, eggs, scallion and cayenne and mix until well combined.
2. Place the mixture into a greased 6x2-inch cake pan.
3. Arrange the "Crisper Basket" in the pot of Ninja Air Smart XL Indoor Grill.
4. Close the Ninja Air Smart XL Indoor Grill with lid and select "Air Crisp".
5. Set the temperature to 360 degrees F to preheat.
6. Press "Start/Stop" to begin preheating.
7. When the display shows "Add Food" open the lid and place the pan into the "Crisper Basket".
8. Close the Ninja Air Smart XL Indoor Grill with lid and set the time for 20 minutes.
9. Press "Start/Stop" to begin cooking.
10. When the cooking time is completed, press "Start/Stop" to stop cooking.
11. Open the lid and serve hot.

Nutritional Information per Serving:

- Calories 437
- Total Fat 34.2 g
- Saturated Fat 13.9 g
- Cholesterol 405 mg
- Sodium 726 mg
- Total Carbs 2.2 g
- Fiber 0.4 g
- Sugar 1.2 g
- Protein 29.4 g

Mushroom Frittata

Preparation Time: 15 minutes
Cooking Time: 14 minutes
Servings: 2
Ingredients:

- 1 tablespoon olive oil
- 1 bacon slice, chopped
- 6 cherry tomatoes, halved
- 6 fresh mushrooms, sliced
- Salt and ground black pepper, as required

- 3 eggs
- ½ cup Parmesan cheese, grated
- 1 tablespoon fresh parsley, chopped

Method:

1. In a baking dish, add the bacon, tomatoes, mushrooms, salt, and black pepper and mix well.
2. Arrange the "Crisper Basket" in the pot of Ninja Air Smart XL Indoor Grill.
3. Close the Ninja Air Smart XL Indoor Grill with lid and select "Air Crisp".
4. Set the temperature to 320 degrees F to preheat.
5. Press "Start/Stop" to begin preheating.
6. When the display shows "Add Food" open the lid and place the baking dish into the "Crisper Basket".
7. Close the Ninja Air Smart XL Indoor Grill with lid and set the time for 6 minutes.
8. Press "Start/Stop" to begin cooking.
9. Meanwhile, in a bowl, add the eggs and beat well.
10. Add in the parsley and cheese and mix well.
11. After 6 minutes, top the bacon mixture with egg mixture evenly.
12. Close the Ninja Air Smart XL Indoor Grill with lid and set the time for 8 minutes.
13. When the cooking time is completed, press "Start/Stop" to stop cooking.
14. Open the lid and serve hot.

Nutritional Information per Serving:

- Calories 489
- Total Fat 35.8 g
- Saturated Fat 15.1 g
- Cholesterol 321 mg
- Sodium 1950 mg
- Total Carbs 7.5 g
- Fiber 0.9 g
- Sugar 2.1 g
- Protein 39.6 g

Bacon & Kale Casserole

Preparation Time: 10 minutes
Cooking Time: 17 minutes
Servings: 6
Ingredients:

- 6 eggs
- ½ cup milk
- Salt and ground black pepper, as required

- 1 cup fresh kale, tough ribs removed and chopped
- 4 cooked bacon slices, crumbled

Method:

1. Arrange the "Crisper Basket" in the pot of Ninja Air Smart XL Indoor Grill.
2. Close the Ninja Air Smart XL Indoor Grill with lid and select "Air Crisp".
3. Set the temperature to 325 degrees F to preheat.
4. Press "Start/Stop" to begin preheating.
5. In a bowl, add the eggs, milk, salt and black pepper and beat until well combined.
6. Add the kale and stir to combine.
7. Divide the kale mixture into 6 greased cups.
8. When the display shows "Add Food" open the lid and place the cups into the "Crisper Basket".
9. Close the Ninja Air Smart XL Indoor Grill with lid and set the time for 17 minutes.
10. Press "Start/Stop" to begin cooking.
11. When the cooking time is completed, press "Start/Stop" to stop cooking.
12. Open the lid and transfer the frittata onto a platter.
13. Cut into equal-sized wedges and serve with the topping of bacon pieces.

Nutritional Information per Serving:

- Calories 183
- Total Fat 12.9 g
- Saturated Fat 4.3 g
- Cholesterol 187 mg
- Sodium 550 mg
- Total Carbs 2.8 g
- Fiber 0.2 g
- Sugar 1.3 g
- Protein 13.7 g

Turkey & Cheddar Casserole

Preparation Time: 10 minutes
Cooking Time: 25 minutes
Servings: 4
Ingredients:

- 6 eggs
- ½ cup plain Greek yogurt
- ½ cup cooked turkey meat, chopped
- Salt and ground black pepper, as required
- ½ cup sharp cheddar cheese, shredded

Method:

1. Arrange the "Crisper Basket" in the pot of Ninja Air Smart XL Indoor Grill.
2. Close the Ninja Air Smart XL Indoor Grill with lid and select "Bake".
3. Set the temperature to 375 degrees F to preheat.
4. Press "Start/Stop" to begin preheating.
5. In a bowl, add the egg and yogurt and beat well.
6. Add the remaining ingredients and stir to combine.
7. In the greased baking pan, place the egg mixture.
8. When the display shows "Add Food" open the lid and place the pan into the "Crisper Basket".
9. Close the Ninja Air Smart XL Indoor Grill with lid and set the time for 25 minutes.
10. Press "Start/Stop" to begin cooking.
11. When the cooking time is completed, press "Start/Stop" to stop cooking.
12. Open the lid and transfer the casserole onto a platter.
13. Cut into equal-sized wedges and serve hot.

Nutritional Information per Serving:

- Calories 203
- Total Fat 12.4 g
- Saturated Fat 5.6 g
- Cholesterol 275 mg
- Sodium 253 mg
- Total Carbs 2.9 g
- Fiber 0 g
- Sugar 2.7 g
- Protein 18.7 g

Savory Carrot Muffins

Preparation Time: 15 minutes
Cooking Time: 7 minutes
Servings: 6
Ingredients:

- ¼ cup whole-wheat flour
- ¼ cup all-purpose flour
- ½ teaspoon baking powder
- 1/8 teaspoon baking soda
- ½ teaspoon dried parsley, crushed
- ¼ teaspoon salt
- ½ cup yogurt
- 1 teaspoon balsamic vinegar
- 1 tablespoon vegetable oil
- 3 tablespoons cottage cheese, grated
- 1 carrot, peeled and grated
- 2-4 tablespoons water (if needed)

- 7 ounces Parmesan cheese, grated
- ¼ cup walnuts, chopped

Method:

1. Grease 6 medium muffin molds.
2. In a large bowl, mix together the flours, baking powder, baking soda, parsley, and salt.
3. In another large bowl, add the yogurt and vinegar and mix well.
4. Add the oil, cottage cheese and carrot and mix well. (Add some water if needed).
5. Make a well in the center of the yogurt mixture.
6. Slowly, add the flour mixture in the well and mix until well combined.
7. Place the mixture into the prepared muffin molds evenly and top with the Parmesan cheese and walnuts.
8. Arrange the "Crisper Basket" in the pot of Ninja Air Smart XL Indoor Grill.
9. Close the Ninja Air Smart XL Indoor Grill with lid and select "Air Crisp".
10. Set the temperature to 355 degrees F to preheat.
11. Press "Start/Stop" to begin preheating.
12. When the display shows "Add Food" open the lid and place the muffin molds into the "Crisper Basket".
13. Close the Ninja Air Smart XL Indoor Grill with lid and set the time for 7 minutes.
14. Press "Start/Stop" to begin cooking.
15. When the cooking time is completed, press "Start/Stop" to stop cooking.
16. Open the lid and place the muffin molds onto a wire rack for about 10 minutes.
17. Carefully, invert the muffins onto the wire rack to cool completely before serving.

Nutritional Information per Serving:

- Calories 222
- Total Fat 12.9 g
- Saturated Fat 5.7 g
- Cholesterol 25 mg
- Sodium 482 mg
- Total Carbs 12.6 g
- Fiber 0.9 g
- Sugar 2 g
- Protein 15.2 g

Banana Bread

Preparation Time: 10 minutes
Cooking Time: 20 minutes
Servings: 8
Ingredients:

- 1 1/3 cups flour
- 2/3 cup sugar
- 1 teaspoon baking soda
- 1 teaspoon baking powder
- 1 teaspoon ground cinnamon
- ¼ teaspoon salt
- ½ cup milk
- ½ cup olive oil
- 3 bananas, peeled and sliced

Method:

1. In the bowl of a stand mixer, add all the ingredients and mix until well combined.
2. Place the mixture into a greased loaf pan.
3. Arrange the "Crisper Basket" in the pot of Ninja Air Smart XL Indoor Grill.
4. Close the Ninja Air Smart XL Indoor Grill with lid and select "Air Crisp".
5. Set the temperature to 330 degrees F to preheat.
6. Press "Start/Stop" to begin preheating.
7. When the display shows "Add Food" open the lid and place the loaf pan into the "Crisper Basket".
8. Close the Ninja Air Smart XL Indoor Grill with lid and set the time for 20 minutes.
9. Press "Start/Stop" to begin cooking.
10. When the cooking time is completed, press "Start/Stop" to stop cooking.
11. Open the lid and place the pan onto a wire rack for about 10-15 minutes.
12. Carefully, invert the bread onto the wire rack to cool completely before slicing.
13. Cut the bread into desired size slices and serve.

Nutritional Information per Serving:

- Calories 295
- Total Fat 13.3 g
- Saturated Fat 2.1 g
- Cholesterol 1 mg
- Sodium 241 mg
- Total Carbs 44 g
- Fiber 1.9 g
- Sugar 22.8 g
- Protein 3.1 g

Pumpkin Bread

Preparation Time: 15 minutes
Cooking Time: 25 minutes
Servings: 4
Ingredients:

- ¼ cup coconut flour
- 2 tablespoons stevia blend

- 1 teaspoon baking powder
- ¾ teaspoon pumpkin pie spice
- ¼ teaspoon ground cinnamon
- 1/8 teaspoon salt
- ¼ cup canned pumpkin
- 2 large eggs
- 2 tablespoons unsweetened almond milk
- 1 teaspoon vanilla extract

Method:

1. In a bowl, add the flour, stevia blend, baking powder, spices and salt and mix well.
2. In another large bowl, add the pumpkin, eggs, almond milk, and vanilla extract. Beat until well combined.
3. Add the flour mixture and mix until just combined.
4. Arrange the "Crisper Basket" in the pot of Ninja Air Smart XL Indoor Grill.
5. Close the Ninja Air Smart XL Indoor Grill with lid and select "Air Crisp".
6. Set the temperature to 350 degrees F to preheat.
7. Press "Start/Stop" to begin preheating.
8. Place the mixture into a greased parchment paper lined cake pan evenly.
9. When the display shows "Add Food" open the lid and place the pan into the "Crisper Basket".
10. Close the Ninja Air Smart XL Indoor Grill with lid and set the time for 25 minutes.
11. Press "Start/Stop" to begin cooking.
12. When the cooking time is completed, press "Start/Stop" to stop cooking.
13. Open the lid and place the bread pan onto a wire rack for about 5-10 minutes.
14. Carefully, remove the bread from pan and place onto a wire rack to cool completely before slicing.
15. Cut the bread into desired-sized slices and serve.

Nutritional Information per Serving:

- Calories 78
- Total Fat 3.4 g
- Saturated Fat 1.3 g
- Cholesterol 93 mg
- Sodium 116 mg
- Total Carbs 7.5 g
- Fiber 3.6 g
- Sugar 0.9 g
- Protein 4.4 g

Chapter 4: Meat Recipes

Buttered Beef Steaks

Preparation Time: 10 minutes

Cooking Time: 8 minutes

Servings: 4

Ingredients:

- 2 (14-ounce) New York strip steaks
- 2 tablespoons butter, melted
- Salt and ground black pepper, as required

Method:

1. Brush each steak with the melted butter and season with salt and black pepper.
2. Arrange the "Grill Grate" in the pot of Ninja Air Smart XL Indoor Grill.
3. Close the Ninja Air Smart XL Indoor Grill with lid and select "Grill" to "High" for 5 minutes.
4. Press "Start/Stop" to begin preheating.
5. When the display shows "Add Food" open the lid and place the steaks onto the "Grill Grate".
6. With your hands, gently press down each steak.
7. Close the Ninja Air Smart XL Indoor Grill with lid and set the time for 8 minutes.
8. Press "Start/Stop" to begin cooking.
9. After 4 minutes of cooking, flip the steaks.
10. When the cooking time is completed, press "Start/Stop" to stop cooking.
11. Open the lid and transfer the steaks onto a cutting board for about 5 minutes before slicing.
12. Cut each steak into 2 portions and serve.

Nutritional Information per Serving:

- Calories 296
- Total Fat 12.7 g
- Saturated Fat 6.6 g
- Cholesterol 115 mg
- Sodium 226 mg
- Total Carbs 0 g
- Fiber 0 g
- Sugar 0 g
- Protein 44.5 g

Crispy Sirloin Steaks

Preparation Time: 15 minutes
Cooking Time: 14 minutes
Servings: 3
Ingredients:

- ½ cup flour
- Salt and ground black pepper, as required
- 2 eggs
- ¾ cup breadcrumbs
- 3 (6-ounce) sirloin steaks, pounded

Method:

1. In a shallow bowl, place the flour, salt and black pepper and mix well.
2. In a second shallow bowl, beat the eggs.
3. In a third shallow bowl, place the breadcrumbs.
4. Coat the steak with flour, then dip into eggs, and finally coat with the panko mixture.
5. Arrange the "Crisper Basket" in the pot of Ninja Air Smart XL Indoor Grill.
6. Close the Ninja Air Smart XL Indoor Grill with lid and select "Air Crisp".
7. Set the temperature to 360 degrees F to preheat.
8. Press "Start/Stop" to begin preheating.
9. When the display shows "Add Food" open the lid and place the steaks into the "Crisper Basket".
10. Close the Ninja Air Smart XL Indoor Grill with lid and set the time for 14 minutes.
11. Press "Start/Stop" to begin cooking.
12. When the cooking time is completed, press "Start/Stop" to stop cooking.
13. Open the lid and serve hot.

Nutritional Information per Serving:

- Calories 540
- Total Fat 15.2 g
- Saturated Fat 5.3 g
- Cholesterol 261 mg
- Sodium 402 mg
- Total Carbs 35.6 g
- Fiber 1.8 g
- Sugar 2 g
- Protein 61 g

Seasoned Filet Mignon

Preparation Time: 10 minutes
Cooking Time: 7 minutes
Servings: 4
Ingredients:

- 4 (8-ounce) filet mignon
- ¼ cup olive oil
- 2 tablespoons steak seasoning
- 1 tablespoon salt

Method:

1. Coat both sides of each filet mignon with oil and then rub with steak seasoning and salt.
2. Arrange the "Grill Grate" in the pot of Ninja Air Smart XL Indoor Grill.
3. Close the Ninja Air Smart XL Indoor Grill with lid and select "Grill" to "High" for 5 minutes.
4. With your hands, gently press down each fillet mignon.
5. Press "Start/Stop" to begin preheating.
6. When the display shows "Add Food" open the lid and place the filets onto the "Grill Grate".
7. Close the Ninja Air Smart XL Indoor Grill with lid and set the time for 8 minutes.
8. Press "Start/Stop" to begin cooking.
9. After 4 minutes, flip the filets.
10. When the cooking time is completed, press "Start/Stop" to stop cooking.
11. Open the lid and transfer the filets onto a platter for about 5 minutes before serving.

Nutritional Information per Serving:

- Calories 425
- Total Fat 16.7 g
- Saturated Fat 6.1 g
- Cholesterol 150 mg
- Sodium 1800 mg
- Total Carbs 0.8 g
- Fiber 0.6 g
- Sugar 0.1 g
- Protein 63.9 g

Bacon-Wrapped Beef Tenderloin

Preparation Time: 15 minutes

Cooking Time: 12 minutes

Servings: 4

Ingredients:

- 8 bacon strips
- 4 (8-ounce) center-cut beef tenderloin filets
- 2 tablespoons 0live oil, divided
- Salt and ground black pepper, as required

Method:

1. Wrap 2 bacon strips around the entire outside of each beef filet.
2. With toothpicks, secure each filet.
3. Coat each wrapped filet with oil and sprinkle with salt and black pepper evenly.
4. Arrange the "Grill Grate" in the pot of Ninja Air Smart XL Indoor Grill.
5. Close the Ninja Air Smart XL Indoor Grill with lid and select "Grill" to "High" for 5 minutes.
6. Press "Start/Stop" to begin preheating.
7. When the display shows "Add Food" open the lid and place the wrapped filets onto the "Grill Grate".
8. Close the Ninja Air Smart XL Indoor Grill with lid and set the time for 12 minutes.
9. Press "Start/Stop" to begin cooking.
10. After 6 minutes of cooking, flip the filets.
11. When the cooking time is completed, press "Start/Stop" to stop cooking.
12. Open the lid and transfer the filets onto a platter for about 10 minutes before serving.

Nutritional Information per Serving:

- Calories 841
- Total Fat 52 g
- Saturated Fat 16.9 g
- Cholesterol 272 mg
- Sodium 1500 mg
- Total Carbs 0.8 g
- Fiber 0 g
- Sugar 1 g
- Protein 87.1 g

Bacon-Wrapped Beef Tenderloin

Preparation Time: 15 minutes

Cooking Time: 12 minutes

Servings: 4

Ingredients:

- 8 bacon strips
- 4 (8-ounce) center-cut beef tenderloin filets
- 2 tablespoons Olive oil, divided
- Salt and ground black pepper, as required

Method:

1. Wrap 2 bacon strips around the entire outside of each beef filet.
2. With toothpicks, secure each filet.
3. Coat each wrapped filet with oil and sprinkle with salt and black pepper evenly.
4. Arrange the "Grill Grate" in the pot of Ninja Air Smart XL Indoor Grill.
5. Close the Ninja Air Smart XL Indoor Grill with lid and select "Grill" to "High" for 5 minutes.
6. Press "Start/Stop" to begin preheating.
7. When the display shows "Add Food" open the lid and place the wrapped filets onto the "Grill Grate".
8. Close the Ninja Air Smart XL Indoor Grill with lid and set the time for 12 minutes.
9. Press "Start/Stop" to begin cooking.
10. After 6 minutes of cooking, flip the filets.
11. When the cooking time is completed, press "Start/Stop" to stop cooking.
12. Open the lid and transfer the filets onto a platter for about 10 minutes before serving.

Nutritional Information per Serving:

- Calories 841
- Total Fat 52 g
- Saturated Fat 16.9 g
- Cholesterol 272 mg
- Sodium 1500 mg
- Total Carbs 0.8 g
- Fiber 0 g
- Sugar 1 g
- Protein 87.1 g

Crumbed Steak

Preparation Time: 10 minutes
Cooking Time: 10 minutes
Servings: 2
Ingredients:

- 1 cup white flour
- 2 eggs

- 1 cup panko breadcrumbs
- 1 teaspoon garlic powder
- 1 teaspoon onion powder
- Salt and ground black pepper, as required
- 2 (6-ounce) sirloin steaks, pounded slightly

Method:

1. In a shallow bowl, place the flour.
2. Crack the eggs in a second bowl and beat well.
3. In a third bowl, mix together the panko and spices.
4. Coat each steak with the flour, then dip into beaten eggs and finally, coat with panko mixture.
5. Arrange the greased "Crisper Basket" in the pot of Ninja Air Smart XL Indoor Grill.
6. Close the Ninja Air Smart XL Indoor Grill with lid and select "Air Crisp".
7. Set the temperature to 360 degrees F to preheat.
8. Press "Start/Stop" to begin preheating.
9. When the display shows "Add Food" open the lid and place the steaks into the "Crisper Basket".
10. Close the Ninja Air Smart XL Indoor Grill with lid and set the time for 10 minutes.
11. Press "Start/Stop" to begin cooking.
12. When the cooking time is completed, press "Start/Stop" to stop cooking.
13. Open the lid and serve hot.

Nutritional Information per Serving:

- Calories 810
- Total Fat 19.4 g
- Saturated Fat 7 g
- Cholesterol 316 mg
- Sodium 253 mg
- Total Carbs 58.2 g
- Fiber 2.1 g
- Sugar 1.4 g
- Protein 65.4 g

Garlicky Lamb Chops

Preparation Time: 15 minutes
Cooking Time: 15 minutes
Servings: 4
Ingredients:

- 4 garlic cloves, crushed
- 1 tablespoon fresh lemon juice
- 1 teaspoon olive oil
- 1 tablespoon Za'atar
- Kosher salt and ground black pepper, as required
- 8 (3½-ounces) bone-in lamb loin chops, trimmed

Method:

1. In a large bowl, mix together the garlic, lemon juice, oil, Za'atar, salt and black pepper.
2. Coat the chops with the garlic mixture
3. Arrange the greased "Crisper Basket" in the pot of Ninja Air Smart XL Indoor Grill.
4. Close the Ninja Air Smart XL Indoor Grill with lid and select "Air Crisp".
5. Set the temperature to 400 degrees F to preheat.
6. Press "Start/Stop" to begin preheating.
7. When the display shows "Add Food" open the lid and place the chops into the "Crisper Basket".
8. Close the Ninja Air Smart XL Indoor Grill with lid and set the time for 15 minutes.
9. Press "Start/Stop" to begin cooking.
10. Flip the chops once halfway through.
11. When the cooking time is completed, press "Start/Stop" to stop cooking.
12. Open the lid and serve hot.

Nutritional Information per Serving:

- Calories 385
- Total Fat 15.8 g
- Saturated Fat 5.4 g
- Cholesterol 179 mg
- Sodium 191 mg
- Total Carbs 1.1 g
- Fiber 0.1 g
- Sugar 0.1 g
- Protein 55.9 g

Sweet & Sour Lamb Chops

Preparation Time: 15 minutes
Cooking Time: 40 minutes
Servings: 3
Ingredients:

- 3 (8-ounce) lamb shoulder chops

- Salt and ground black pepper, as required
- ¼ cup sugar
- 2 tablespoons fresh lime juice

Method:

1. Season the lamb chops with salt and black pepper generously.in a baking pan, place the chops and sprinkle with Sugar, followed by the lime juice.
2. Arrange the "Crisper Basket" in the pot of Ninja Air Smart XL Indoor Grill.
3. Close the Ninja Foodi with crisping lid and select "Roast".
4. Set the temperature to 376 degrees F to preheat.
5. Press "Start/Stop" to begin preheating.
6. After preheating, open the lid and place the lamb chops into the "Crisper Basket".
7. Close the Ninja Foodi with crisping lid and set the time for 40 minutes.
8. Press "Start/Stop" to begin cooking.
9. After 20 minutes of cooking, flip the chops and coat with the pan juices.
10. When the cooking time is completed, press "Start/Stop" to stop cooking.
11. Open the lid and serve hot.

Nutritional Information per Serving:

- Calories 405
- Total Fat 18.1 g
- Saturated Fat 6 g
- Cholesterol 151 mg
- Sodium 211 mg
- Total Carbs 16.8 g
- Fiber 0 g
- Sugar 16.7 g
- Protein 44.2 g

Pesto Rack of Lamb

Preparation Time: 15 minutes
Cooking Time: 15 minutes
Servings: 4
Ingredients:

- ½ bunch fresh mint
- 1 garlic clove
- ¼ cup extra-virgin olive oil
- ½ tablespoons honey
- Salt and ground black pepper, as required
- 1 (1½-pound) rack of lamb

Method:

1. For pesto: in a blender, add the mint, garlic, oil, honey, salt, and black pepper and pulse until smooth.

2. Coat the rack of lamb with some pesto evenly.
3. Arrange the greased "Crisper Basket" in the pot of Ninja Air Smart XL Indoor Grill.
4. Close the Ninja Air Smart XL Indoor Grill with lid and select "Air Crisp".
5. Set the temperature to 200 degrees F to preheat.
6. Press "Start/Stop" to begin preheating.
7. When the display shows "Add Food" open the lid and place the rack of lamb into the "Crisper Basket".
8. Close the Ninja Air Smart XL Indoor Grill with lid and set the time for 15 minutes.
9. Press "Start/Stop" to begin cooking.
10. While cooking, coat the rack of lamb with the remaining pesto after every 5 minutes.
11. When the cooking time is completed, press "Start/Stop" to stop cooking.
12. Open the lid and place the rack of lamb onto a cutting board for about 5 minutes.
13. Cut the rack into individual chops and serve.

Nutritional Information per Serving:

- Calories 405
- Total Fat 27.7 g
- Saturated Fat 7.1 g
- Cholesterol 113 mg
- Sodium 161 mg
- Total Carbs 2.8 g
- Fiber 0.3 g
- Sugar 2.2 g
- Protein 34.8 g

Almond Crusted Rack of Lamb

Preparation Time: 15 minutes
Cooking Time: 35 minutes
Servings: 6
Ingredients:

- 1 (1¾-pound) rack of lamb
- Salt and ground black pepper, as required
- 1 egg
- 1 tablespoon breadcrumbs
- 3 ounces almonds, chopped finely

Method:

1. Season the rack of lamb with salt and black pepper evenly and then, drizzle with cooking spray.

2. In a shallow dish, beat the egg.
3. In another shallow dish, mix together the breadcrumbs and almonds.
4. Dip the rack of lamb in egg and then coat with the almond mixture.
5. Arrange the "Crisper Basket" in the pot of Ninja Air Smart XL Indoor Grill.
6. Close the Ninja Air Smart XL Indoor Grill with lid and select "Air Crisp".
7. Set the temperature to 220 degrees F to preheat.
8. Press "Start/Stop" to begin preheating.
9. When the display shows "Add Food" open the lid and place the rack of lamb into the "Crisper Basket".
10. Close the Ninja Air Smart XL Indoor Grill with lid and set the time for 30 minutes.
11. Press "Start/Stop" to begin cooking.
12. After 30 minutes, set the temperature to 390 degrees F to preheat.
13. When the cooking time is completed, press "Start/Stop" to stop cooking.
14. Open the lid and place the rack of lamb onto a cutting board for about 5 minutes.
15. Cut the rack into individual chops and serve.

Nutritional Information per Serving:

- Calories 319
- Total Fat 19.6 g
- Saturated Fat 4.9 g
- Cholesterol 115 mg
- Sodium 139 mg
- Total Carbs 3.9 g
- Fiber 1.8 g
- Sugar 0.7 g
- Protein 31 g

Simple Pork Chops

Preparation Time: 10 minutes
Cooking Time: 18 minutes
Servings: 2
Ingredients:

- 2 (6-ounce) (½-inch thick) pork chops
- Salt and ground black pepper, as required

Method:

1. Season the both sides of the pork chops with salt and black pepper generously.
2. Arrange the pork chops onto a greased baking pan.
3. Arrange the "Grill Grate" in the pot of Ninja Air Smart XL Indoor Grill.

4. Close the Ninja Air Smart XL Indoor Grill with lid and select "Grill" on "Medium" for 5 minutes.
5. Press "Start/Stop" to begin preheating.
6. When the display shows "Add Food" open the lid and place the baking pan onto the "Grill Grate".
7. With your hands, gently press down each pork chop.
8. Close the Ninja Air Smart XL Indoor Grill with lid and set the time for 18 minutes.
9. Press "Start/Stop" to begin cooking.
10. After 12 minutes of cooking, flip the chops once.
11. When the cooking time is completed, press "Start/Stop" to stop cooking.
12. Open the lid and serve hot.

Nutritional Information per Serving:

- Calories 544
- Total Fat 42.3 g
- Saturated Fat 15.8 g
- Cholesterol 147 mg
- Sodium 197 mg
- Total Carbs 0 g
- Fiber 0 g
- Sugar 0 g
- Protein 38.2 g

Sweet & Sour Pork Chops

Preparation Time: 10 minutes
Cooking Time: 16 minutes
Servings: 6
Ingredients:

- 6 pork loin chops
- Salt and ground black pepper, as required
- 2 tablespoons honey
- 2 tablespoons soy sauce
- 1 tablespoon balsamic vinegar

Method:
1. With a meat tenderizer, tenderize the chops completely.
2. Sprinkle the chops with a little salt and black pepper.
3. In a large bowl, place the remaining ingredients and mix well.
4. Add the chops and coat with marinade generously.
5. Refrigerate, covered for about 6-8 hours.
6. Arrange the "Crisper Basket" in the pot of Ninja Air Smart XL Indoor Grill.

7. Close the Ninja Air Smart XL Indoor Grill with lid and select "Air Crisp".
8. Set the temperature to 355 degrees F to preheat.
9. Press "Start/Stop" to begin preheating.
10. When the display shows "Add Food" open the lid and place the pork chops into the "Crisper Basket".
11. Close the Ninja Air Smart XL Indoor Grill with lid and set the time for 16 minutes.
12. Press "Start/Stop" to begin cooking.
13. After 8 minutes of cooking, flip the chops.
14. When the cooking time is completed, press "Start/Stop" to stop cooking.
15. Open the lid and serve hot.

Nutritional Information per Serving:

- Calories 569
- Total Fat 42.3 g
- Saturated Fat 15.8 g
- Cholesterol 146 mg
- Sodium 447 mg
- Total Carbs 6.2 g
- Fiber 0.1 g
- Sugar 5.9 g
- Protein 38.6 g

BBQ Pork Chops

Preparation Time: 10 minutes
Cooking Time: 16 minutes
Servings: 6
Ingredients:

- 6 (8-ounce) pork loin chops
- Salt and ground black pepper, as required
- ½ cup BBQ sauce

Method:
1. With a meat tenderizer, tenderize the chops completely.
2. Sprinkle the chops with a little salt and black pepper.
3. In a large bowl, add the BBQ sauce and chops and mix well.
4. Refrigerate, covered for about 6-8 hours.
5. Arrange the "Crisper Basket" in the pot of Ninja Air Smart XL Indoor Grill.
6. Close the Ninja Air Smart XL Indoor Grill with lid and select "Air Crisp".
7. Set the temperature to 355 degrees F to preheat.

8. Press "Start/Stop" to begin preheating.
9. When the display shows "Add Food" open the lid and place the chops into the "Crisper Basket".
10. Close the Ninja Air Smart XL Indoor Grill with lid and set the time for 16 minutes.
11. Press "Start/Stop" to begin cooking.
12. After 8 minutes of cooking, flip the chops.
13. When the cooking time is completed, press "Start/Stop" to stop cooking.
14. Open the lid and serve hot.

Nutritional Information per Serving:

- Calories 757
- Total Fat 56.4 g
- Saturated Fat 21.1 g
- Cholesterol 195 mg
- Sodium 419 mg
- Total Carbs 7.6 g
- Fiber 0.1 g
- Sugar 5.4 g
- Protein 51 g

Stuffed Pork Roll

Preparation Time: 20 minutes
Cooking Time: 15 minutes
Servings: 4

Ingredients:

- 1 scallion, chopped
- ¼ cup sun-dried tomatoes, chopped finely
- 2 tablespoons fresh parsley, chopped
- Salt and ground black pepper, as required
- 4 (6-ounce) pork cutlets, pounded slightly
- 2 teaspoons paprika
- ½ tablespoons olive oil

Method:

1. In a bowl, mix together the scallion, tomatoes, parsley, salt, and black pepper.
2. Spread the tomato mixture over each pork cutlet.
3. Roll each cutlet and secure with cocktail sticks.
4. Rub the outer part of rolls with paprika, salt and black pepper.
5. Coat the rolls with oil evenly.

6. Arrange the greased "Crisper Basket" in the pot of Ninja Air Smart XL Indoor Grill.
7. Close the Ninja Air Smart XL Indoor Grill with lid and select "Air Crisp".
8. Set the temperature to 390 degrees F to preheat.
9. Press "Start/Stop" to begin preheating.
10. When the display shows "Add Food" open the lid and place the pork rolls into the "Crisper Basket" in a single layer.
11. Close the Ninja Air Smart XL Indoor Grill with lid and set the time for 15 minutes.
12. Press "Start/Stop" to begin cooking.
13. When the cooking time is completed, press "Start/Stop" to stop cooking.
14. Open the lid and serve hot.

Nutritional Information per Serving:

- Calories 244
- Total Fat 14.5 g
- Saturated Fat 2.7 g
- Cholesterol 15 mg
- Sodium 708 mg
- Total Carbs 20.1 g
- Fiber 2.6 g
- Sugar 1.7 g
- Protein 8.2 g

Chapter 5: Poultry Recipes

Roasted Whole Chicken

Preparation Time: 10 minutes
Cooking Time: 1 hour
Servings: 2
Ingredients:

- 1 (1½-pound) whole chicken
- Salt and ground black pepper, as required
- 1 tablespoon dried rosemary, crushed

Method:

1. Arrange the greased "Crisper Basket" in the pot of Ninja Air Smart XL Indoor Grill.
2. Close the Ninja Air Smart XL Indoor Grill with lid and select "Air Crisp".
3. Set the temperature to 390 degrees F to preheat.
4. Press "Start/Stop" to begin preheating.
5. Season the chicken with salt and black pepper and then rub with rosemary.
6. When the display shows "Add Food" open the lid and place the chicken into the "Crisper Basket".
7. Close the Ninja Air Smart XL Indoor Grill with lid and set the time for 60 minutes.
8. Press "Start/Stop" to begin cooking.
9. When the cooking time is completed, press "Start/Stop" to stop cooking.
10. Open the lid and place the chicken onto a cutting board for about 10 minutes.
11. Cut the chicken into desired size pieces and serve alongside the potatoes.

Nutritional Information per Serving:

- Calories 638
- Total Fat 24.5 g
- Saturated Fat 12.1 g
- Cholesterol 289 mg
- Sodium 351 mg
- Total Carbs 0 g
- Fiber 0 g
- Sugar 0 g
- Protein 60.8 g

BBQ Chicken Breasts

Preparation Time: 10 minutes
Cooking Time: 22 minutes
Servings: 4

Ingredients:

- 4 (8-ounce) frozen boneless, skinless chicken breasts
- 2 tablespoons olive oil, divided
- Salt and ground black pepper, as required
- 1 cup BBQ sauce

Method:

1. Brush the chicken breasts with ½ tablespoon of oil evenly and season with salt and black pepper.
2. Arrange the "Grill Grate" in the pot of Ninja Air Smart XL Indoor Grill.
3. Close the Ninja Air Smart XL Indoor Grill with lid and select "Grill" to "Medium" for 5 minutes.
4. Press "Start/Stop" to begin preheating.
5. When the display shows "Add Food" open the lid and place the chicken breasts onto the "Grill Grate".
6. With your hands, gently press down the chicken breasts.
7. Close the Ninja Air Smart XL Indoor Grill with lid and set the time for 10 minutes.
8. Press "Start/Stop" to begin cooking.
9. After 10 minutes, flip the chicken breasts.
10. Close the Ninja Air Smart XL Indoor Grill with lid and set the time for 5 minutes.
11. After 5 minutes, flip the chicken breasts and coat the upper side with barbecue sauce generously.
12. Close the Ninja Air Smart XL Indoor Grill with lid and set the time for 5 minutes from the remaining cooking time.
13. After 5 minutes, flip the chicken breasts and coat the upper side with barbecue sauce generously.
14. Close the Ninja Air Smart XL Indoor Grill with lid and set the time for 2 minutes.
15. When the cooking time is completed, press "Start/Stop" to stop cooking.
16. Open the lid and place the chicken breasts onto a platter and set aside for about 5 minutes before serving.

Nutritional Information per Serving:

- Calories 585
- Total Fat 24 g
- Saturated Fat 5.6 g
- Cholesterol 202 mg
- Sodium 933 mg
- Total Carbs 22.7 g
- Fiber 0.4 g
- Sugar 16.3 g
- Protein 65.6 g

Spiced Chicken Breasts

Preparation Time: 10 minutes
Cooking Time: 35 minutes
Servings: 4
Ingredients:

- 1½ tablespoons smoked paprika
- 1 teaspoon ground cumin
- Salt and ground black pepper, as required
- 2 (12-ounce) bone-in, skin-on chicken breasts
- 1 tablespoon olive oil

Method:

1. In a small bowl, mix together the paprika, cumin, salt and black pepper.
2. Coat the chicken breasts with oil evenly and then season with the spice mixture generously.
3. Arrange the "Crisper Basket" in the pot of Ninja Air Smart XL Indoor Grill.
4. Close the Ninja Air Smart XL Indoor Grill with lid and select "Air Crisp".
5. Set the temperature to 375 degrees F to preheat.
6. Press "Start/Stop" to begin preheating.
7. When the display shows "Add Food" open the lid and place the chicken breasts into the "Crisper Basket".
8. Close the Ninja Air Smart XL Indoor Grill with lid and set the time for 35 minutes.
9. Press "Start/Stop" to begin cooking.
10. When the cooking time is completed, press "Start/Stop" to stop cooking.
11. Open the lid and place the chicken breasts onto a cutting board for about 5 minutes.
12. Cut each breast in 2 equal-sized pieces and serve.

Nutritional Information per Serving:

- Calories 363
- Total Fat 16.6 g
- Saturated Fat 4 g
- Cholesterol 151 mg
- Sodium 187 mg
- Total Carbs 1.7 g
- Fiber 1 g
- Sugar 0.3 g
- Protein 49.7 g

Oat Crusted Chicken Breasts

Preparation Time: 15 minutes
Cooking Time: 12 minutes
Servings: 2
Ingredients:

- 2 (6-ounce) chicken breasts
- Salt and ground black pepper, as required
- ¾ cup oats
- 2 tablespoons mustard powder
- 1 tablespoon fresh parsley
- 2 medium eggs

Method:

1. Place the chicken breasts onto a cutting board and with a meat mallet, flatten each into even thickness.
2. Then, cut each breast in half.
3. Sprinkle the chicken pieces with salt and black pepper and set aside.
4. In a blender, add the oats, mustard powder, parsley, salt and black pepper and pulse until a coarse breadcrumb-like mixture is formed.
5. Transfer the oat mixture into a shallow bowl.
6. In another bowl, crack the eggs and beat well.
7. Coat the chicken with oats mixture and then, dip into beaten eggs and again, coat with the oats mixture.
8. Arrange the "Crisper Basket" in the pot of Ninja Air Smart XL Indoor Grill.
9. Close the Ninja Air Smart XL Indoor Grill with lid and select "Air Crisp".
10. Set the temperature to 350 degrees F to preheat.
11. Press "Start/Stop" to begin preheating.
12. When the display shows "Add Food" open the lid and place the chicken breasts into the "Crisper Basket".
13. Close the Ninja Air Smart XL Indoor Grill with lid and set the time for 12 minutes.

14. Press "Start/Stop" to begin cooking.
15. While cooking, flip the chicken breasts once halfway through.
16. When the cooking time is completed, press "Start/Stop" to stop cooking.
17. Open the lid and place the chicken breasts onto a cutting board for about 5 minutes before serving.

Nutritional Information per Serving:

- Calories 556
- Total Fat 22.2 g
- Saturated Fat 5.3 g
- Cholesterol 315 mg
- Sodium 289 mg
- Total Carbs 25.1 g
- Fiber 4.8 g
- Sugar 1.40 g
- Protein 61.6 g

Lemony Chicken Thighs

Preparation Time: 15 minutes
Cooking Time: 20 minutes
Servings: 6
Ingredients:

- 6 (6-ounce) chicken thighs
- 2 tablespoons olive oil
- 2 tablespoons fresh lemon juice
- 1 tablespoon Italian seasoning
- Salt and ground black pepper, as required
- 1 lemon, sliced thinly

Method:

1. In a large bowl, add all the ingredients except for lemon slices and toss to coat well.
2. Refrigerate to marinate for 30 minutes to overnight.
3. Remove the chicken thighs and let any excess marinade drip off.
4. Arrange the "Crisper Basket" in the pot of Ninja Air Smart XL Indoor Grill.
5. Close the Ninja Air Smart XL Indoor Grill with lid and select "Air Crisp".
6. Set the temperature to 350 degrees F to preheat.
7. Press "Start/Stop" to begin preheating.
8. When the display shows "Add Food" open the lid and place the chicken thighs into the "Crisper Basket".
9. Close the Ninja Air Smart XL Indoor Grill with lid and set the time for 20 minutes.
10. Press "Start/Stop" to begin cooking.

11. After 10 minutes of cooking, flip the chicken thighs.
12. When the cooking time is completed, press "Start/Stop" to stop cooking.
13. Open the lid and transfer the chicken thighs onto serving plates.
14. Serve hot alongside the lemon slices.

Nutritional Information per Serving:

- Calories 372
- Total Fat 18 g
- Saturated Fat 4.3 g
- Cholesterol 153 mg
- Sodium 175 mg
- Total Carbs 0.6 g
- Fiber 0.1 g
- Sugar 0.4 g
- Protein 49.3 g

Marinated Chicken Thighs

Preparation Time: 10 minutes
Cooking Time: 30 minutes
Servings: 4
Ingredients:

- 4 (6-ounce) bone-in, skin-on chicken thighs
- Salt and ground black pepper, as required
- ½ cup Italian salad dressing
- 1 teaspoon onion powder
- 1 teaspoon garlic powder

Method:

1. Season the chicken thighs with salt and black pepper evenly.
2. In a large bowl, add the chicken thighs and dressing and mix well.
3. Cover the bowl and refrigerate to marinate overnight.
4. Remove the chicken breast from the bowl and place onto a plate.
5. Sprinkle the chicken thighs with onion powder and garlic powder.
6. Arrange the "Crisper Basket" in the pot of Ninja Air Smart XL Indoor Grill.
7. Close the Ninja Air Smart XL Indoor Grill with lid and select "Air Crisp".
8. Set the temperature to 360 degrees F to preheat.
9. Press "Start/Stop" to begin preheating.
10. When the display shows "Add Food" open the lid and place the chicken thighs into the "Crisper Basket".
11. Close the Ninja Air Smart XL Indoor Grill with lid and set the time for 30 minutes.

12. Press "Start/Stop" to begin cooking.
13. After 15 minutes of cooking, flip the chicken thighs.
14. When the cooking time is completed, press "Start/Stop" to stop cooking.
15. Open the lid and transfer the chicken thighs onto serving plates.
16. Serve hot.

Nutritional Information per Serving:

- Calories 413
- Total Fat 21 g
- Saturated Fat 4.8 g
- Cholesterol 171 mg
- Sodium 194 mg

- Total Carbs 4.1 g
- Fiber 0.1 g
- Sugar 2.8 g
- Protein 49.5 g

Sweet & Spicy Chicken Drumsticks

Preparation Time: 15 minutes
Cooking Time: 20 minutes
Servings: 4
Ingredients:

- 1 garlic clove, crushed
- 1 teaspoon cayenne pepper
- 1 teaspoon red chili powder
- 2 teaspoons sugar

- 1 tablespoon mustard
- Salt and ground black pepper, as required
- 1 tablespoon olive oil
- 4 (6-ounce) chicken drumsticks

Method:

1. In a bowl, mix together all ingredients except chicken drumsticks.
2. Rub the chicken with the oil mix and refrigerate to marinate for about 20-30 minutes.
3. Arrange the greased "Crisper Basket" in the pot of Ninja Air Smart XL Indoor Grill.
4. Close the Ninja Air Smart XL Indoor Grill with lid and select "Air Crisp".
5. Set the temperature to 390 degrees F to preheat.
6. Press "Start/Stop" to begin preheating.
7. When the display shows "Add Food" open the lid and place the chicken drumsticks into the "Crisper Basket".

8. Close the Ninja Air Smart XL Indoor Grill with lid and set the time for 10 minutes.
9. Press "Start/Stop" to begin cooking.
10. After 10 minutes of cooking, set the temperature to 300 degrees F for 10 minutes.
11. When the cooking time is completed, press "Start/Stop" to stop cooking.
12. Open the lid and serve hot.

Nutritional Information per Serving:

- Calories 343
- Total Fat 14.2 g
- Saturated Fat 3.1 g
- Cholesterol 150 mg
- Sodium 182 mg
- Total Carbs 3.8 g
- Fiber 0.8 g
- Sugar 2.3 g
- Protein 47.7 g

Glazed Chicken Drumsticks

Preparation Time: 15 minutes
Cooking Time: 20 minutes
Servings: 4
Ingredients:

- ¼ cup Dijon mustard
- 1 tablespoon honey
- 2 tablespoons olive oil
- 1 tablespoon fresh thyme, minced
- ½ tablespoon fresh rosemary, minced
- Salt and ground black pepper, as required
- 4 (6-ounce) boneless chicken drumsticksMarinated the chicken drumsticks with all the above ingredients for overnight.Preheat Philips Airfryer at 160 degree.

Method:
1. In a Baked the drumstick for 12 minutes at 160 degree. Then baked for 5 to 10 minutes at 180 degree for crispy skin.bowl, add all ingredients except the drumsticks and mix until well combined.
2. Add the drumsticks and coat with the mixture generously.
3. Refrigerate, covered to marinate overnight.
4. Arrange the lightly greased "Crisper Basket" in the pot of Ninja Air Smart XL Indoor Grill.
5. Close the Ninja Air Smart XL Indoor Grill with lid and select "Air Crisp".

6. Set the temperature to 320 degrees F to preheat.
7. Press "Start/Stop" to begin preheating.
8. When the display shows "Add Food" open the lid and place the chicken drumsticks into the "Crisper Basket".
9. Close the Ninja Air Smart XL Indoor Grill with lid and set the time for 12 minutes.
10. Press "Start/Stop" to begin cooking.
11. After 12 minutes, flip the drumsticks and set the temperature to 390 degrees F for 8 minutes.
12. When the cooking time is completed, press "Start/Stop" to stop cooking.
13. Open the lid and serve hot.

Nutritional Information per Serving:

- Calories 377
- Total Fat 17.5 g
- Saturated Fat 3.7 g
- Cholesterol 150 mg
- Sodium 372 mg
- Total Carbs 5.9 g
- Fiber 1 g
- Sugar 4.5 g
- Protein 47.6 g

Crispy Chicken Legs

Preparation Time: 15 minutes
Cooking Time: 20 minutes
Servings: 3
Ingredients:

- 3 (8-ounce) chicken legs
- 1 cup buttermilk
- 2 cups white flour
- 1 teaspoon garlic powder
- 1 teaspoon onion powder
- 1 teaspoon ground cumin
- 1 teaspoon paprika
- Salt and ground black pepper, as required
- 1 tablespoon olive oil

Method:
1. In a bowl, place the chicken legs and buttermilk and refrigerate for about 2 hours.
2. In a shallow dish, mix together the flour and spices.
3. Remove the chicken from buttermilk.
4. Coat the chicken legs with flour mixture, then dip into buttermilk and finally, coat with the flour mixture again.

5. Arrange the greased "Crisper Basket" in the pot of Ninja Air Smart XL Indoor Grill.
6. Close the Ninja Air Smart XL Indoor Grill with lid and select "Air Crisp".
7. Set the temperature to 360 degrees F to preheat.
8. Press "Start/Stop" to begin preheating.
9. When the display shows "Add Food" open the lid and place the chicken legs into the "Crisper Basket".
10. Close the Ninja Air Smart XL Indoor Grill with lid and set the time for 20 minutes.
11. Press "Start/Stop" to begin cooking.
12. When the cooking time is completed, press "Start/Stop" to stop cooking.
13. Open the lid and serve hot.

Nutritional Information per Serving:

- Calories 817
- Total Fat 23.3 g
- Saturated Fat 5.9 g
- Cholesterol 205 mg
- Sodium 335 mg
- Total Carbs 69.5 g
- Fiber 2.7 g
- Sugar 4.7 g
- Protein 77.4 g

Spicy Chicken Legs

Preparation Time: 15 minutes
Cooking Time: 20 minutes
Servings: 4
Ingredients:

- 4 (8-ounce) chicken legs
- 3 tablespoons fresh lemon juice
- 3 teaspoons ginger paste
- 3 teaspoons garlic paste
- Salt, as required
- 4 tablespoons plain yogurt
- 2 teaspoons red chili powder
- 1 teaspoon ground cumin
- 1 teaspoon ground coriander
- 1 teaspoon ground turmeric
- Ground black pepper, as required

Method:

1. In a bowl, mix together the chicken legs, lemon juice, ginger, garlic and salt. Set aside for about 15 minutes.
2. Meanwhile, in another bowl, mix together the yogurt and spices.

3. Add the chicken legs and coat with the spice mixture generously.
4. Cover the bowl and refrigerate for at least 10-12 hours.
5. Arrange the greased "Crisper Basket" in the pot of Ninja Air Smart XL Indoor Grill.
6. Close the Ninja Air Smart XL Indoor Grill with lid and select "Air Crisp".
7. Set the temperature to 445 degrees F to preheat.
8. Press "Start/Stop" to begin preheating.
9. When the display shows "Add Food" open the lid and place the chicken legs into the "Crisper Basket".
10. Close the Ninja Air Smart XL Indoor Grill with lid and set the time for 20 minutes.
11. Press "Start/Stop" to begin cooking.
12. When the cooking time is completed, press "Start/Stop" to stop cooking.
13. Open the lid and serve hot.

Nutritional Information per Serving:

- Calories 461
- Total Fat 17.6 g
- Saturated Fat 5 g
- Cholesterol 203 mg
- Sodium 262 mg
- Total Carbs 4.3 g
- Fiber 0.9 g
- Sugar 1.5 g
- Protein 67.1 g

Glazed Turkey Breasts

Preparation Time: 15 minutes
Cooking Time: 55 minutes
Servings: 10
Ingredients:

- 1 (5-pound) boneless turkey breast
- Salt and ground black pepper, as required
- 3 tablespoons honey
- 2 tablespoon Dijon mustard
- 1 tablespoon butter, softened

Method:

1. Season the turkey breast with salt and black pepper generously and spray with cooking spray.
2. Arrange the greased "Crisper Basket" in the pot of Ninja Air Smart XL Indoor Grill.

3. Close the Ninja Air Smart XL Indoor Grill with lid and select "Air Crisp".
4. Set the temperature to 350 degrees F to preheat.
5. Press "Start/Stop" to begin preheating.
6. When the display shows "Add Food" open the lid and place the turkey breast into the "Crisper Basket".
7. Close the Ninja Air Smart XL Indoor Grill with lid and set the time for 55 minutes.
8. Press "Start/Stop" to begin cooking.
9. Meanwhile, for glaze: in a bowl, mix together the maple syrup, mustard and butter.
10. Flip the turkey breast twice, first after 25 minutes and then after 37 minutes.
11. After 50 minutes of cooking, coat the turkey breast with the glaze.
12. When the cooking time is completed, press "Start/Stop" to stop cooking.
13. Open the lid and place the turkey breast onto a cutting board for about 5 minutes before slicing.
14. Cut into desired sized slices and serve.

Nutritional Information per Serving:

- Calories 252
- Total Fat 2.3 g
- Saturated Fat 0.7 g
- Cholesterol 144 mg
- Sodium 170 mg
- Total Carbs 5.4 g
- Fiber 0.1 g
- Sugar 5.2 g
- Protein 56.4 g

Herbed Turkey Breast

Preparation Time: 15 minutes
Cooking Time: 35 minutes
Servings: 3
Ingredients:

- 1 teaspoon dried thyme, crushed
- 1 teaspoon dried rosemary, crushed
- ½ teaspoon dried sage, crushed
- ½ teaspoon dark brown sugar
- ½ teaspoon garlic powder
- ½ teaspoon paprika
- Salt and ground black pepper, as required
- 1 (2½-pound) bone-in, skin-on turkey breast
- 1 tablespoon olive oil

Method:

1. In a bowl, mix together the herbs, brown sugar, spices, salt and black pepper.
2. Coat the turkey breast with oil and then rub with the herb mixture evenly.
3. Arrange the "Crisper Basket" in the pot of Ninja Air Smart XL Indoor Grill.
4. Close the Ninja Air Smart XL Indoor Grill with lid and select "Air Crisp".
5. Set the temperature to 360 degrees F to preheat.
6. Press "Start/Stop" to begin preheating.
7. When the display shows "Add Food" open the lid and place the turkey breasts, skin-side down into the "Crisper Basket".
8. Close the Ninja Air Smart XL Indoor Grill with lid and set the time for 35 minutes.
9. Press "Start/Stop" to begin cooking.
10. Flip the turkey breast once after 18 minutes of cooking.
11. When the cooking time is completed, press "Start/Stop" to stop cooking.
12. Open the lid and place the turkey breast onto a cutting board for about 10 minutes before slicing.
13. With a sharp knife, cut the turkey breast into desired sized slices and serve.

Nutritional Information per Serving:

- Calories 440
- Total Fat 11.1 g
- Saturated Fat 2 g
- Cholesterol 163 mg
- Sodium 2000 mg
- Total Carbs 17.5 g
- Fiber 2.4 g
- Sugar 13.9 g
- Protein 64.7 g

Lemony Turkey Legs

Preparation Time: 15 minutes
Cooking Time: 30 minutes
Servings: 2
Ingredients:

- 2 garlic cloves, minced
- 1 tablespoon fresh rosemary, minced
- 1 teaspoon fresh lime zest, finely grated
- 2 tablespoons olive oil
- 1 tablespoon fresh lime juice
- Salt and ground black pepper, as required
- 2 turkey legs

Method:

1. In a large bowl, mix together the garlic, rosemary, lime zest, oil, lime juice, salt, and black pepper.
2. Add the turkey legs and generously coat with marinade.
3. Refrigerate to marinate for about 6-8 hours.
4. Arrange the greased "Crisper Basket" in the pot of Ninja Air Smart XL Indoor Grill.
5. Close the Ninja Air Smart XL Indoor Grill with lid and select "Air Crisp".
6. Set the temperature to 350 degrees F to preheat.
7. Press "Start/Stop" to begin preheating.
8. When the display shows "Add Food" open the lid and place the turkey legs into the "Crisper Basket".
9. Close the Ninja Air Smart XL Indoor Grill with lid and set the time for 30 minutes.
10. Press "Start/Stop" to begin cooking.
11. Flip the turkey legs once halfway through.
12. When the cooking time is completed, press "Start/Stop" to stop cooking.
13. Open the lid and serve hot.

Nutritional Information per Serving:

- Calories 709
- Total Fat 32.7 g
- Saturated Fat 7.8 g
- Cholesterol 238 mg
- Sodium 351mg
- Total Carbs 2.3 g
- Fiber 0.9 g
- Sugar 0.1 g
- Protein 97.2 g

Glazed Duck Breasts

Preparation Time: 15 minutes
Cooking Time: 20 minutes
Servings: 2
Ingredients:

- 1 (10½-ounce) duck breast
- 1 tablespoon wholegrain mustard
- 1 teaspoon honey
- 1 teaspoon balsamic vinegar
- Salt and ground black pepper, as required

Method:

1. Arrange the "Crisper Basket" in the pot of Ninja Air Smart XL Indoor Grill.

2. Close the Ninja Air Smart XL Indoor Grill with lid and select "Air Crisp".
3. Set the temperature to 365 degrees F to preheat.
4. Press "Start/Stop" to begin preheating.
5. When the display shows "Add Food" open the lid and place the duck breast, skin side up into the "Crisper Basket".
6. Close the Ninja Air Smart XL Indoor Grill with lid and set the time for 20 minutes.
7. Press "Start/Stop" to begin cooking.
8. Meanwhile, in a bowl, mix together the remaining ingredients.
9. After 15 minutes of cooking, coat the duck breast with the honey mixture generously.
10. When the cooking time is completed, press "Start/Stop" to stop cooking.
11. Open the lid and serve hot.

Nutritional Information per Serving:

- Calories 229
- Total Fat 7.6 g
- Saturated Fat 0.1 g
- Cholesterol 0 mg
- Sodium 78 mg
- Total Carbs 4.9 g
- Fiber 0.8 g
- Sugar 3.3 g
- Protein 34.2 g

Garlicky Duck Legs

Preparation Time: 10 minutes
Cooking Time: 30 minutes
Servings: 2
Ingredients:

- 2 garlic cloves, minced
- 1 tablespoon fresh parsley, chopped
- 1 teaspoon five spice powder
- Salt and ground black pepper, as required
- 2 duck legs

Method:

1. In a bowl, mix together the garlic, parsley, five spice powder, salt and black pepper.
2. Rub the duck legs with garlic mixture generously.
3. Arrange the "Crisper Basket" in the pot of Ninja Air Smart XL Indoor Grill.
4. Close the Ninja Air Smart XL Indoor Grill with lid and select "Air Crisp".
5. Set the temperature to 340 degrees F to preheat.

6. Press "Start/Stop" to begin preheating.
7. When the display shows "Add Food" open the lid and place the duck legs into the "Crisper Basket".
8. Close the Ninja Air Smart XL Indoor Grill with lid and set the time for 25 minutes.
9. Press "Start/Stop" to begin cooking.
10. After 25 minutes, set the temperature to 390 degrees F to preheat.
11. When the cooking time is completed, press "Start/Stop" to stop cooking.
12. Open the lid and serve hot.

Nutritional Information per Serving:

- Calories 434
- Total Fat 14.4 g
- Saturated Fat 3.2 g
- Cholesterol 253 mg
- Sodium 262 mg
- Total Carbs 1.1 g
- Fiber 0.1 g
- Sugar 0.1 g
- Protein 70.4 g

Chapter 6: Fish & Seafood Recipes

Cajun Salmon

Preparation Time: 10 minutes
Cooking Time: 8 minutes
Servings: 2
Ingredients:

- 2 (6-ounce) salmon steaks
- 2 tablespoons Cajun seasoning

Method:

1. Rub the salmon steaks with the Cajun seasoning evenly and set aside for about 10 minutes.
2. Arrange the "Crisper Basket" in the pot of Ninja Air Smart XL Indoor Grill.
3. Close the Ninja Air Smart XL Indoor Grill with lid and select "Air Crisp".
4. Set the temperature to 390 degrees F to preheat.
5. Press "Start/Stop" to begin preheating.
6. When the display shows "Add Food" open the lid and place the salmon steaks into the "Crisper Basket".
7. Close the Ninja Air Smart XL Indoor Grill with lid and set the time for 8 minutes.
8. Press "Start/Stop" to begin cooking.
9. After 4 minutes of cooking, flip the salmon steaks.
10. When the cooking time is completed, press "Start/Stop" to stop cooking.
11. Open the lid and serve hot.

Nutritional Information per Serving:

- Calories 225
- Total Fat 10.5 g
- Saturated Fat 1.5 g
- Cholesterol 75 mg
- Sodium 225 mg
- Total Carbs 0 g
- Fiber 0 g
- Sugar 0 g
- Protein 22.1 g

Buttered Salmon

Preparation Time: 10 minutes
Cooking Time: 10 minutes
Servings: 2

Ingredients:

- 2 (6-ounce) salmon fillets
- Salt and ground black pepper, as required
- ¼ teaspoon dried rosemary, crushed
- 1 tablespoon butter, melted

Method:

1. Arrange the greased "Crisper Basket" in the pot of Ninja Air Smart XL Indoor Grill.
2. Close the Ninja Air Smart XL Indoor Grill with lid and select "Air Crisp".
3. Set the temperature to 360 degrees F to preheat.
4. Press "Start/Stop" to begin preheating.
5. Season each salmon fillet with salt and black pepper and then sprinkle with rosemary evenly.
6. Now, coat each fillet with the melted butter.
7. When the display shows "Add Food" open the lid and place the salmon fillets into the "Crisper Basket" in a single layer.
8. Close the Ninja Air Smart XL Indoor Grill with lid and set the time for 10 minutes.
9. Press "Start/Stop" to begin cooking.
10. When the cooking time is completed, press "Start/Stop" to stop cooking.
11. Open the lid and serve hot.

Nutritional Information per Serving:

- Calories 276
- Total Fat 16.3 g
- Saturated Fat 5.2 g
- Cholesterol 90 mg
- Sodium 193 mg
- Total Carbs 0 g
- Fiber 0 g
- Sugar 0 g
- Protein 33.1 g

Zesty Salmon

Preparation Time: 10 minutes
Cooking Time: 8 minutes
Servings: 4
Ingredients:

- 1½ pounds salmon fillets
- ½ teaspoon red chili powder
- Salt and ground black pepper, as required

- 1 lime, cut into slices
- 1 tablespoon fresh dill, chopped

Method:

1. Arrange the greased "Crisper Basket" in the pot of Ninja Air Smart XL Indoor Grill.
2. Close the Ninja Air Smart XL Indoor Grill with lid and select "Air Crisp".
3. Set the temperature to 375 degrees F to preheat.
4. Press "Start/Stop" to begin preheating.
5. Season the salmon with chili powder, salt, and black pepper evenly.
6. When the display shows "Add Food" open the lid and place the salmon fillets into the "Crisper Basket".
7. Close the Ninja Air Smart XL Indoor Grill with lid and set the time for 8 minutes.
8. Press "Start/Stop" to begin cooking.
9. When the cooking time is completed, press "Start/Stop" to stop cooking.
10. Open the lid and serve hot with the garnishing of dill.

Nutritional Information per Serving:

- Calories 229
- Total Fat 10.6 g
- Saturated Fat 1.5 g
- Cholesterol 75 mg
- Sodium 119 mg
- Total Carbs 1 g
- Fiber 0.3 g
- Sugar 0.1 g
- Protein 33.2 g

Spicy Catfish

Preparation Time: 15 minutes
Cooking Time: 13 minutes
Servings: 2

Ingredients:

- 2 tablespoons almond flour
- 1 teaspoon red chili powder
- ½ teaspoon paprika
- ½ teaspoon garlic powder
- Salt, as required
- 2 (6-ounces) catfish fillets
- 1 tablespoon olive oil

Method:

1. Arrange the greased "Crisper Basket" in the pot of Ninja Air Smart XL Indoor Grill.
2. Close the Ninja Air Smart XL Indoor Grill with lid and select "Air Crisp".

3. Set the temperature to 400 degrees F to preheat.
4. Press "Start/Stop" to begin preheating.
5. In a bowl, mix together the flour, paprika, garlic powder and salt.
6. Add the catfish fillets and coat with the mixture evenly.
7. Now, coat each fillet with oil.
8. When the display shows "Add Food" open the lid and place the catfish fillets into the "Crisper Basket".
9. Close the Ninja Air Smart XL Indoor Grill with lid and set the time for 13 minutes.
10. Press "Start/Stop" to begin cooking.
11. Flip the fish fillets once halfway through.
12. When the cooking time is completed, press "Start/Stop" to stop cooking.
13. Open the lid and serve hot.

Nutritional Information per Serving:

- Calories 458
- Total Fat 34.2 g
- Saturated Fat 4.4 g
- Cholesterol 80 mg
- Sodium 191 mg
- Total Carbs 7.5 g
- Fiber 3.7 g
- Sugar 1.3 g
- Protein 32.8 g

Seasoned Catfish

Preparation Time: 10 minutes
Cooking Time: 20 minutes
Servings: 4
Ingredients:

- 4 (4-ounce) catfish fillets
- ¼ cup Louisiana fish fry seasoning
- 1 tablespoon olive oil
- 1 tablespoon fresh parsley, chopped

Method:

1. Rub the fish fillets with seasoning generously and then, coat with oil.
2. Arrange the "Crisper Basket" in the pot of Ninja Air Smart XL Indoor Grill.
3. Close the Ninja Air Smart XL Indoor Grill with lid and select "Air Crisp".
4. Set the temperature to 400 degrees F to preheat.
5. Press "Start/Stop" to begin preheating.

6. When the display shows "Add Food" open the lid and place the fish fillets into the "Crisper Basket".
7. Close the Ninja Air Smart XL Indoor Grill with lid and set the time for 20 minutes.
8. Press "Start/Stop" to begin cooking.
9. After 10 minutes of cooking, flip the fish fillets.
10. When the cooking time is completed, press "Start/Stop" to stop cooking.
11. Open the lid and serve hot with the garnishing of parsley.

Nutritional Information per Serving:

- Calories 213
- Total Fat 12.1 g
- Saturated Fat 2.1 g
- Cholesterol 53 mg
- Sodium 263 mg
- Total Carbs 7.6 g
- Fiber 0 g
- Sugar 0 g
- Protein 17.7 g

Glazed Haddock

Preparation Time: 15 minutes
Cooking Time: 15 minutes
Servings: 4
Ingredients:

- 1 garlic clove, minced
- ¼ teaspoon fresh ginger, grated finely
- ½ cup low-sodium soy sauce
- ¼ cup fresh orange juice
- 2 tablespoons fresh lime juice
- ½ cup cooking wine
- ¼ cup sugar
- ¼ teaspoon red pepper flakes, crushed
- 1 pound haddock steaks

Method:
1. In a pan, add all the ingredients except haddock steaks and bring to a boil.
2. Cook for about 3-4 minutes, stirring continuously.
3. Remove from the heat and set aside to cool.
4. In a reseal able bag, add half of marinade and haddock steaks.
5. Seal the bag and shake to coat well.
6. Refrigerate for about 30 minutes.
7. Remove the fish steaks from bag, reserving the remaining marinade.

8. Arrange the greased "Crisper Basket" in the pot of Ninja Air Smart XL Indoor Grill.
9. Close the Ninja Air Smart XL Indoor Grill with lid and select "Air Crisp".
10. Set the temperature to 390 degrees F to preheat.
11. Press "Start/Stop" to begin preheating.
12. When the display shows "Add Food" open the lid and place the haddock steaks into the "Crisper Basket".
13. Close the Ninja Air Smart XL Indoor Grill with lid and set the time for 11 minutes.
13. Press "Start/Stop" to begin cooking.
14. When the cooking time is completed, press "Start/Stop" to stop cooking.
15. Open the lid and transfer the haddock steak onto a serving platter.
16. Immediately, coat the haddock steak with the remaining glaze and serve.

Nutritional Information per Serving:

- Calories 218
- Total Fat 1.1 g
- Saturated Fat 0.2 g
- Cholesterol 84 mg
- Sodium 1860 mg
- Total Carbs 17.4 g
- Fiber 0.1 g
- Sugar 16.1 g
- Protein 29.7 g

Buttered Halibut

Preparation Time: 15 minutes
Cooking Time: 25 minutes
Servings: 4
Ingredients:

- 1 pound halibut fillets
- 1 tablespoon ginger paste
- 1 tablespoon garlic paste
- Salt and ground black pepper, as required
- 3 jalapeño peppers, chopped
- ¾ cup butter, chopped

Method:
1. Coat the halibut fillets with ginger-garlic paste and then, season with salt and black pepper.
2. Close the Ninja Air Smart XL Indoor Grill with lid and select "Roast".
3. Set the temperature to 360 degrees F to preheat.

4. Press "Start/Stop" to begin preheating.
5. When the display shows "Add Food" open the lid and arrange the roasting rack in the pot.
6. Arrange the halibut fillets over the rack and top with jalapeño peppers, followed by the butter.
7. Close the Ninja Air Smart XL Indoor Grill with lid and set the time for 25 minutes.
8. Press "Start/Stop" to begin cooking.
9. When the cooking time is completed, press "Start/Stop" to stop cooking.
10. Open the lid and serve hot.

Nutritional Information per Serving:

- Calories 443
- Total Fat 37.4 g
- Saturated Fat 22.2 g
- Cholesterol 128 mg
- Sodium 620 mg
- Total Carbs 2.5 g
- Fiber 0.6 g
- Sugar 0.5 g
- Protein 24.6 g

Teriyaki Halibut

Preparation Time: 10 minutes
Cooking Time: 8 minutes
Servings: 4
Ingredients:

- 4 (6-ounce) skinless halibut fillets
- 1 cup teriyaki marinade

Method:

1. In a bowl, place all the halibut fillets and teriyaki marinade and mix well.
2. Refrigerate, covered to marinate for about 2-3 hours.
3. Arrange the "Grill Grate" in the pot of Ninja Air Smart XL Indoor Grill.
4. Close the Ninja Air Smart XL Indoor Grill with lid and select "Grill" to "Max" for 5 minutes.
5. Press "Start/Stop" to begin preheating.
6. When the display shows "Add Food" open the lid and place the halibut fillets onto the "Grill Grate".
7. With your hands, gently press down each fillet.
8. Close the Ninja Air Smart XL Indoor Grill with lid and set the time for 8 minutes.

9. Press "Start/Stop" to begin cooking.
10. After 6 minutes of cooking, flip the salmon fillets.
11. When the cooking time is completed, press "Start/Stop" to stop cooking.
12. Open the lid and serve hot.

Nutritional Information per Serving:

- Calories 269
- Total Fat 4 g
- Saturated Fat 0.5 g
- Cholesterol 55 mg
- Sodium 1130 mg
- Total Carbs 16 g
- Fiber 0 g
- Sugar 12 g
- Protein 33 g

Simple Cod

Preparation Time: 10 minutes
Cooking Time: 10 minutes
Servings: 2
Ingredients:

- 2 (6-ounce) cod fillets
- Salt and ground black pepper, as required

Method:

1. Season the cod fillets with salt and black pepper.
2. Arrange the "Grill Grate" in the pot of Ninja Air Smart XL Indoor Grill.
3. Close the Ninja Air Smart XL Indoor Grill with lid and select "Grill" on "Medium" for 5 minutes.
4. Press "Start/Stop" to begin preheating.
5. When the display shows "Add Food" open the lid and grease the "Grill Grate".
6. Place the cod fillets onto the "Grill Grate".
7. With your hands, gently press down each cod fillet.
8. Close the Ninja Air Smart XL Indoor Grill with lid and set the time for 12 minutes.
9. Press "Start/Stop" to begin cooking.
10. When the cooking time is completed, press "Start/Stop" to stop cooking.
11. Open the lid and serve hot.

Nutritional Information per Serving:

- Calories 137
- Total Fat 1.5 g

- Saturated Fat 0 g
- Cholesterol 84 mg
- Sodium 184 mg
- Total Carbs 0 g

- Fiber 0 g
- Sugar 0 g
- Protein 30.4 g

Crispy Cod

Preparation Time: 15 minutes
Cooking Time: 15 minutes
Servings: 4
Ingredients:

- 4 (4-ounce) (¾-inch thick) cod fillets
- Salt, as required
- 2 tablespoons all-purpose flour
- 2 eggs
- ½ cup panko breadcrumbs
- 1 teaspoon fresh dill, minced

- ½ teaspoon dry mustard
- ½ teaspoon lemon zest, grated
- ½ teaspoon onion powder
- ½ teaspoon paprika
- Olive oil cooking spray

Method:

1. Season the cod fillets with salt pepper generously.
2. In a shallow bowl, place the flour.
3. Crack the eggs in a second bowl and beat well.
4. In a third bowl, mix together the panko, dill, lemon zest, mustard and spices.
5. Coat each cod fillet with the flour, then dip into beaten eggs and finally, coat with panko mixture.
6. Arrange the greased "Crisper Basket" in the pot of Ninja Air Smart XL Indoor Grill.
7. Close the Ninja Air Smart XL Indoor Grill with lid and select "Air Crisp".
8. Set the temperature to 400 degrees F to preheat.
9. Press "Start/Stop" to begin preheating.
10. When the display shows "Add Food" open the lid and place the cod fillets into the "Crisper Basket".
11. Spray the cod fillets with cooking spray.
12. Close the Ninja Air Smart XL Indoor Grill with lid and set the time for 15 minutes.
13. Press "Start/Stop" to begin cooking.

14. While cooking, flip the cod fillets once hallway through and spray with cooking spray.
15. When the cooking time is completed, press "Start/Stop" to stop cooking.
16. Open the lid and serve hot.

Nutritional Information per Serving:

- Calories 190
- Total Fat 4.3 g
- Saturated Fat 1.1 g
- Cholesterol 138 mg
- Sodium 141 mg
- Total Carbs 5.9 g
- Fiber 0.4 g
- Sugar 0.4 g
- Protein 24 g

Cod & Veggie Parcel

Preparation Time: 20 minutes
Cooking Time: 15 minutes
Servings: 2

Ingredients:

- 2 tablespoons butter, melted
- 1 tablespoon fresh lemon juice
- ½ teaspoon dried tarragon
- Salt and ground black pepper, as required
- ½ cup red bell peppers, seeded and sliced thinly
- ½ cup carrots, peeled and julienned
- ½ cup fennel bulbs, julienned
- 2 (5-ounce) frozen cod fillets, thawed
- 1 tablespoon olive oil

Method:

1. In a large bowl, place the butter, lemon juice, tarragon, salt, and black pepper and mix well.
2. Add the bell pepper, carrot, and fennel bulb and coat with the mixture generously.
3. Arrange 2 large parchment squares onto a smooth surface.
4. Coat the cod fillets with oil and then, sprinkle evenly with salt and black pepper.
5. Arrange 1 cod fillet onto each parchment square and top each with the vegetables evenly.
6. Top with any remaining sauce from the bowl.
7. Fold the parchment paper and crimp the sides to secure fish and vegetables.
8. Arrange the "Crisper Basket" in the pot of Ninja Air Smart XL Indoor Grill.
9. Close the Ninja Air Smart XL Indoor Grill with lid and select "Air Crisp".

10. Set the temperature to 350 degrees F to preheat.
11. Press "Start/Stop" to begin preheating.
12. When the display shows "Add Food" open the lid and place the fish parcels into the "Crisper Basket".
13. Close the Ninja Air Smart XL Indoor Grill with lid and set the time for 15 minutes.
14. Press "Start/Stop" to begin cooking.
15. When the cooking time is completed, press "Start/Stop" to stop cooking.
16. Open the lid and transfer the parcels onto serving plates.
17. Carefully, open each parcel and serve warm.

Nutritional Information per Serving:

- Calories 306
- Total Fat 20 g
- Saturated Fat 8.4 g
- Cholesterol 100 mg
- Sodium 281 mg
- Total Carbs 6.8 g
- Fiber 1.8 g
- Sugar 3 g
- Protein 26.3 g

Lemony Shrimp

Preparation Time: 15 minutes
Cooking Time: 8 minutes
Servings: 3
Ingredients:

- 2 tablespoons fresh lemon juice
- 1 tablespoon olive oil
- 1 teaspoon lemon pepper
- ¼ teaspoon paprika
- ¼ teaspoon garlic powder
- 12 ounces medium shrimp, peeled and deveined

Method:

1. In a large bowl, add all the ingredients except the shrimp and mix until well combined.
2. Add the shrimp and toss to coat well.
3. Arrange the greased "Crisper Basket" in the pot of Ninja Air Smart XL Indoor Grill.
4. Close the Ninja Air Smart XL Indoor Grill with lid and select "Air Crisp".
5. Set the temperature to 400 degrees F to preheat.

6. Press "Start/Stop" to begin preheating.
7. When the display shows "Add Food" open the lid and place the shrimp into the "Crisper Basket".
8. Close the Ninja Air Smart XL Indoor Grill with lid and set the time for 8 minutes.
9. Press "Start/Stop" to begin cooking.
10. When the cooking time is completed, press "Start/Stop" to stop cooking.
11. Open the lid and serve hot.

Nutritional Information per Serving:

- Calories 154
- Total Fat 6.1 g
- Saturated Fat 0.8 g
- Cholesterol 2230 mg
- Sodium 259 mg
- Total Carbs 0.9 g
- Fiber 0.3 g
- Sugar 0.3 g
- Protein 24.5 g

Parmesan Shrimp

Preparation Time: 20 minutes
Cooking Time: 20 minutes
Servings: 4
Ingredients:

- 2/3 cup Parmesan cheese, grated
- 4 garlic cloves, minced
- 2 tablespoons olive oil
- 1 teaspoon dried basil
- ½ teaspoon dried oregano
- 1 teaspoon onion powder
- ½ teaspoon red pepper flakes, crushed
- Ground black pepper, as required
- 2 pounds shrimp, peeled and deveined
- 1-2 tablespoons fresh lemon juice

Method:
1. Arrange the greased "Crisper Basket" in the pot of Ninja Air Smart XL Indoor Grill.
2. Close the Ninja Air Smart XL Indoor Grill with lid and select "Air Crisp".
3. Set the temperature to 350 degrees F to preheat.
4. Press "Start/Stop" to begin preheating.
5. In a large bowl, add the Parmesan cheese, garlic, oil, herbs, and spices and mix well.
6. Add the shrimp and toss to coat well.

7. When the display shows "Add Food" open the lid and place half of the shrimp into the "Crisper Basket" in a single layer.
8. Close the Ninja Air Smart XL Indoor Grill with lid and set the time for 10 minutes.
9. Press "Start/Stop" to begin cooking.
10. When the cooking time is completed, press "Start/Stop" to stop cooking.
11. Open the lid and transfer the shrimp onto a platter.
12. Repeat with the remaining shrimp.
13. Drizzle with lemon juice and serve immediately.

Nutritional Information per Serving:
- Calories 386
- Total Fat 14.2 g
- Saturated Fat 3.8 g
- Cholesterol 488 mg
- Sodium 670 mg
- Total Carbs 5.3 g
- Fiber 0.3 g
- Sugar 0.4 g
- Protein 57.3 g

Buttered Scallops

Preparation Time: 15 minutes
Cooking Time: 4 minutes
Servings: 2
Ingredients:
- ¾ pound sea scallops, cleaned and patted very dry
- 1 tablespoon butter, melted
- ½ tablespoon fresh thyme, minced
- Salt and ground black pepper, as required

Method:
1. In a large bowl, place the scallops, butter, thyme, salt, and black pepper and toss to coat well.
2. Arrange the "Crisper Basket" in the pot of Ninja Air Smart XL Indoor Grill.
3. Close the Ninja Air Smart XL Indoor Grill with lid and select "Air Crisp".
4. Set the temperature to 390 degrees F to preheat.
5. Press "Start/Stop" to begin preheating.
6. When the display shows "Add Food" open the lid and place the scallops into the "Crisper Basket".
7. Close the Ninja Air Smart XL Indoor Grill with lid and set the time for 4 minutes.

8. Press "Start/Stop" to begin cooking.
9. When the cooking time is completed, press "Start/Stop" to stop cooking.
10. Open the lid and serve hot.

Nutritional Information per Serving:

- Calories 135
- Total Fat 4.7 g
- Saturated Fat 2.5 g
- Cholesterol 48 mg
- Sodium 260 mg
- Total Carbs 3 g
- Fiber 0.2 g
- Sugar 0 g
- Protein 19.1 g

Scallops with Spinach

Preparation Time: 15 minutes
Cooking Time: 10 minutes
Servings: 3

Ingredients:

- 1 (10-ounce) package frozen spinach, thawed and drained
- 12 sea scallops
- Olive oil cooking spray
- Salt and ground black pepper, as required
- ¾ cup heavy whipping cream
- 1 tablespoon tomato paste
- 1 teaspoon garlic, minced
- 1 tablespoon fresh basil, chopped

Method:

1. Arrange the greased "Crisper Basket" in the pot of Ninja Air Smart XL Indoor Grill.
2. Close the Ninja Air Smart XL Indoor Grill with lid and select "Air Crisp".
3. Set the temperature to 350 degrees F to preheat.
4. Press "Start/Stop" to begin preheating.
5. In the bottom of a 7-inch heatproof pan, place the spinach.
6. Spray each scallop with cooking spray and then sprinkle with a little salt and black pepper.
7. Arrange scallops on top of the spinach in a single layer.
8. In a bowl, add the cream, tomato paste, garlic, basil, salt and black pepper and mix well.
9. Place the cream mixture over the spinach and scallops evenly.

10. When the display shows "Add Food" open the lid and place the pan into "Crisper Basket".
11. Close the Ninja Air Smart XL Indoor Grill with lid and set the time for 10 minutes.
12. Press "Start/Stop" to begin cooking.
13. When the cooking time is completed, press "Start/Stop" to stop cooking.
14. Open the lid and serve hot.

Nutritional Information per Serving:

- Calories 237
- Total Fat 12.4 g
- Saturated Fat 7.1 g
- Cholesterol 81 mg
- Sodium 335 mg
- Total Carbs 8.4 g
- Fiber 2.3 g
- Sugar 1.1 g
- Protein 23.8 g

Chapter 7: Vegetarian Recipes

Pesto Tomatoes

Preparation Time: 15 minutes
Cooking Time: 14 minutes
Servings: 4
Ingredients:
For Pesto:

- ½ cup olive oil
- 3 tablespoons pine nuts
- Salt, as required
- ½ cup fresh basil, chopped
- ½ cup fresh parsley, chopped
- 1 garlic clove, chopped
- ½ cup Parmesan cheese, grated

For Tomatoes:

- 4 heirloom tomatoes, cut into ½ inch thick slices
- 8 ounces feta cheese, cut into ½ inch thick slices.
- ½ cup red onions, thinly sliced
- 1 tablespoon olive oil
- Salt, as required

Method:

1. In a food processor, add the pine nuts, fresh herbs, garlic, Parmesan, and salt and pulse until just combined.
2. While motor is running, slowly add the oil and pulse until smooth.
3. Transfer the pesto into a bowl, and refrigerate, covered until serving.
4. Spread about one tablespoons of pesto onto each tomato slice.
5. Top each tomato slice with one feta and onion slice and drizzle with oil.
6. Arrange the "Crisper Basket" in the pot of Ninja Air Smart XL Indoor Grill.
7. Close the Ninja Air Smart XL Indoor Grill with lid and select "Air Crisp".
8. Set the temperature to 390 degrees F to preheat.
9. Press "Start/Stop" to begin preheating.
10. When the display shows "Add Food" open the lid and place the scallops into the "Crisper Basket".
11. Close the Ninja Air Smart XL Indoor Grill with lid and set the time for 14 minutes.
12. Press "Start/Stop" to begin cooking.

13. When the cooking time is completed, press "Start/Stop" to stop cooking.
14. Open the lid and transfer the tomato slices onto serving plates.
15. Sprinkle with a little salt and serve with the remaining pesto.

Nutritional Information per Serving:

- Calories 616
- Total Fat 56.3 g
- Saturated Fat 18.3 g
- Cholesterol 80 mg
- Sodium 1000 mg
- Total Carbs 12.1 g
- Fiber 2.4 g
- Sugar 6.5 g
- Protein 22.5 g

Stuffed Tomatoes

Preparation Time: 15 minutes
Cooking Time: 14 minutes
Servings: 2
Ingredients:

- 2 large tomatoes
- ½ cup broccoli, chopped finely
- ½ cup cheddar cheese, shredded
- 1 tablespoon unsalted butter, melted
- ½ teaspoon dried thyme, crushed

Method:

1. Carefully, cut the top of each tomato and scoop out pulp and seeds.
2. In a bowl, place the chopped broccoli and cheese and mix.
3. Stuff each tomato with broccoli mixture evenly.
4. Arrange the "Crisper Basket" in the pot of Ninja Air Smart XL Indoor Grill.
5. Close the Ninja Air Smart XL Indoor Grill with lid and select "Air Crisp".
6. Set the temperature to 355 degrees F to preheat.
7. Press "Start/Stop" to begin preheating.
8. When the display shows "Add Food" open the lid and place the tomatoes into the "Crisper Basket".
9. Drizzle the tomatoes with the butter.
10. Close the Ninja Air Smart XL Indoor Grill with lid and set the time for 15 minutes.
11. Press "Start/Stop" to begin cooking.
12. When the cooking time is completed, press "Start/Stop" to stop cooking.
13. Open the lid and serve with the garnishing of thyme.

Nutritional Information per Serving:

- Calories 206
- Total Fat 15.6 g
- Saturated Fat 9.7 g
- Cholesterol 45 mg
- Sodium 233 mg
- Total Carbs 9.1 g
- Fiber 2.9 g
- Sugar 5.3 g
- Protein 9.4 g

Glazed Carrots

Preparation Time: 10 minutes
Cooking Time: 12 minutes
Servings: 4
Ingredients:

- 3 cups carrots, peeled and cut into large chunks
- 1 tablespoon olive oil
- 1 tablespoon honey
- 1 tablespoon fresh thyme, finely chopped
- Salt and ground black pepper, as required

Method:

1. In a bowl, add the carrot, oil, honey, thyme, salt and black pepper and mix until well combined.
2. Arrange the "Crisper Basket" in the pot of Ninja Air Smart XL Indoor Grill.
3. Close the Ninja Air Smart XL Indoor Grill with lid and select "Air Crisp".
4. Set the temperature to 390 degrees F to preheat.
5. Press "Start/Stop" to begin preheating.
6. When the display shows "Add Food" open the lid and place the carrot chunks into the "Crisper Basket" in a single layer.
7. Close the Ninja Air Smart XL Indoor Grill with lid and set the time for 12 minutes.
8. Press "Start/Stop" to begin cooking.
9. When the cooking time is completed, press "Start/Stop" to stop cooking.
10. Open the lid and serve hot.

Nutritional Information per Serving:

- Calories 82
- Total Fat 3.6 g
- Saturated Fat 0.5 g
- Cholesterol 0 mg
- Sodium 96 mg
- Total Carbs 12.9 g

- Fiber 2.3 g
- Sugar 8.4 g
- Protein 0.8 g

Lemony Green Beans

Preparation Time: 15 minutes
Cooking Time: 12 minutes
Servings: 4
Ingredients:

- 1 pound fresh green beans, trimmed
- 1 tablespoon butter, melted
- 1 tablespoon fresh lemon juice
- ¼ teaspoon garlic powder
- Salt and ground black pepper, as required
- ½ teaspoon lemon zest, grated

Method:
1. In a large bowl, add all the ingredients except the lemon zest and toss to coat well.
2. Arrange the "Crisper Basket" in the pot of Ninja Air Smart XL Indoor Grill.
3. Close the Ninja Air Smart XL Indoor Grill with lid and select "Air Crisp".
4. Set the temperature to 400 degrees F to preheat.
5. Press "Start/Stop" to begin preheating.
6. When the display shows "Add Food" open the lid and place the green beans into the "Crisper Basket".
7. Close the Ninja Air Smart XL Indoor Grill with lid and set the time for 12 minutes.
8. Press "Start/Stop" to begin cooking.
9. When the cooking time is completed, press "Start/Stop" to stop cooking.
10. Open the lid and serve warm with the garnishing of lemon zest.

Nutritional Information per Serving:

- Calories 62
- Total Fat 3.1 g
- Saturated Fat 1.9 g
- Cholesterol 8 mg
- Sodium 67 mg
- Total Carbs 8.4 g
- Fiber 3.9 g
- Sugar 1.7 g
- Protein 2.2 g

Seasoned Zucchini

Preparation Time: 15 minutes
Cooking Time: 10 minutes
Servings: 6

Ingredients:

- 4 large zucchinis, cut into slices
- ¼ cup olive oil
- ½ onion, sliced
- ¾ teaspoon Italian seasoning
- ½ teaspoon garlic salt
- ¼ teaspoon seasoned salt

Method:

1. In a large bowl, mix together all the ingredients.
2. Arrange the greased "Crisper Basket" in the pot of Ninja Air Smart XL Indoor Grill.
3. Close the Ninja Air Smart XL Indoor Grill with lid and select "Air Crisp".
4. Set the temperature to 400 degrees F to preheat.
5. Press "Start/Stop" to begin preheating.
6. When the display shows "Add Food" open the lid and place the zucchini slices into the "Crisper Basket".
7. Close the Ninja Air Smart XL Indoor Grill with lid and set the time for 10 minutes.
8. Press "Start/Stop" to begin cooking.
9. When the cooking time is completed, press "Start/Stop" to stop cooking.
10. Open the lid and serve hot.

Nutritional Information per Serving:

- Calories 106
- Total Fat 8.9 g
- Saturated Fat 1.3 g
- Cholesterol 0 mg
- Sodium 81 mg
- Total Carbs 6.9 g
- Fiber 2.1 g
- Sugar 3.5 g
- Protein 2.2 g

Parmesan Asparagus

Preparation Time: 10 minutes
Cooking Time: 10 minutes

Servings: 3

Ingredients:

- 1 pound fresh asparagus, trimmed
- 1 tablespoon Parmesan cheese, grated
- 1 tablespoon butter, melted
- 1 teaspoon garlic powder
- Salt and ground black pepper, as required

Method:

1. In a bowl, mix together the asparagus, cheese, butter, garlic powder, salt, and black pepper.
2. Arrange the "Crisper Basket" in the pot of Ninja Air Smart XL Indoor Grill.
3. Close the Ninja Air Smart XL Indoor Grill with lid and select "Air Crisp".
4. Set the temperature to 400 degrees F to preheat.
5. Press "Start/Stop" to begin preheating.
6. When the display shows "Add Food" open the lid and place the veggie mixture into the "Crisper Basket".
7. Close the Ninja Air Smart XL Indoor Grill with lid and set the time for 10 minutes.
8. Press "Start/Stop" to begin cooking.
9. When the cooking time is completed, press "Start/Stop" to stop cooking.
10. Open the lid and serve hot.

Nutritional Information per Serving:

- Calories 73
- Total Fat 4.4 g
- Saturated Fat 2.7 g
- Cholesterol 12 mg
- Sodium 95 mg
- Total Carbs 6.6 g
- Fiber 3.3 g
- Sugar 3.1 g
- Protein 4.2 g

Cheesy Spinach

Preparation Time: 15 minutes
Cooking Time: 15 minutes
Servings: 4

Ingredients:

- 1 pound fresh spinach, chopped
- 4 tablespoons butter, melted
- Salt and ground black pepper, as required
- 1 cup feta cheese, crumbled

- 1 teaspoon fresh lemon zest, grated

Method:

1. In a bowl, add the spinach, butter, salt and black pepper and mix well.
2. Arrange the "Crisper Basket" in the pot of Ninja Air Smart XL Indoor Grill.
3. Close the Ninja Air Smart XL Indoor Grill with lid and select "Air Crisp".
4. Set the temperature to 340 degrees F to preheat.
5. Press "Start/Stop" to begin preheating.
6. When the display shows "Add Food" open the lid and place the spinach mixture into the "Crisper Basket".
7. Close the Ninja Air Smart XL Indoor Grill with lid and set the time for 15 minutes.
8. Press "Start/Stop" to begin cooking.
9. When the cooking time is completed, press "Start/Stop" to stop cooking.
10. Open the lid and immediately, transfer the spinach mixture into a bowl.
11. Stir in the cheese and lemon zest and serve hot.

Nutritional Information per Serving:

- Calories 227
- Total Fat 19.9 g
- Saturated Fat 13 g
- Cholesterol 64 mg
- Sodium 629 mg
- Total Carbs 5.8 g
- Fiber 2.5 g
- Sugar 2.1 g
- Protein 8.7 g

Cheesy Mushrooms

Preparation Time: 15 minutes
Cooking Time: 8 minutes
Servings: 2
Ingredients:

- 8 ounces button mushrooms, stemmed
- 2 tablespoons olive oil
- 2 tablespoons Italian dried mixed herbs
- Salt and ground black pepper, as required
- 2 tablespoons mozzarella cheese, grated
- 2 tablespoons cheddar cheese, grated
- 1 teaspoon dried dill

Method:

1. Wash and trim thin slices from the ends of the stems.
2. In a bowl, mix together the mushrooms, dried herbs, oil, salt and black pepper.
3. Arrange the greased "Crisper Basket" in the pot of Ninja Air Smart XL Indoor Grill.
4. Close the Ninja Air Smart XL Indoor Grill with lid and select "Air Crisp".
5. Set the temperature to 355 degrees F to preheat.
6. Press "Start/Stop" to begin preheating.
7. When the display shows "Add Food" open the lid and place the mushrooms hollow part upwards into the "Crisper Basket".
8. Close the Ninja Air Smart XL Indoor Grill with lid and set the time for 8 minutes.
9. Press "Start/Stop" to begin cooking.
10. When the cooking time is completed, press "Start/Stop" to stop cooking.
11. Open the lid and serve with the garnishing of dill.

Nutritional Information per Serving:

- Calories 257
- Total Fat 21.7 g
- Saturated Fat 6.5 g
- Cholesterol 22 mg
- Sodium 299 mg
- Total Carbs 5.8 g
- Fiber 1.7 g
- Sugar 2 g
- Protein 13.6 g

Jacket Potatoes

Preparation Time: 10 minutes
Cooking Time: 15 minutes
Servings: 2
Ingredients:

- 2 potatoes
- 1 tablespoon mozzarella cheese, shredded
- 3 tablespoons sour cream
- 1 tablespoon butter, softened
- 1 teaspoon fresh chives, minced
- Salt and ground black pepper, as required

Method:
1. Arrange the greased "Crisper Basket" in the pot of Ninja Air Smart XL Indoor Grill.
2. Close the Ninja Air Smart XL Indoor Grill with lid and select "Air Crisp".
3. Set the temperature to 355 degrees F to preheat.

4. Press "Start/Stop" to begin preheating.
5. With a fork, prick the potatoes.
6. When the display shows "Add Food" open the lid and place the potatoes into the "Crisper Basket".
7. Close the Ninja Air Smart XL Indoor Grill with lid and set the time for 15 minutes.
8. Press "Start/Stop" to begin cooking.
9. Meanwhile, in a bowl, add the remaining ingredients and mix until well combined.
10. When the cooking time is completed, press "Start/Stop" to stop cooking.
11. Open the lid and transfer the potatoes onto a platter.
12. Open potatoes from the center and stuff them with cheese mixture.
13. Serve immediately

Nutritional Information per Serving:

- Calories 277
- Total Fat 12.2 g
- Saturated Fat 7.6 g
- Cholesterol 31 mg
- Sodium 226 mg
- Total Carbs 34.8 g
- Fiber 5.1 g
- Sugar 2.5 g
- Protein 8.2 g

Stuffed Potatoes

Preparation Time: 15 minutes
Cooking Time: 26 minutes
Servings: 4
Ingredients:

- 4 potatoes, peeled
- 2-3 tablespoons canola oil
- 1 tablespoon butter
- ½ of brown onion, chopped
- 2 tablespoons chives, chopped
- ½ cup Parmesan cheese, grated

Method:

1. Coat the potatoes with some oil.
2. Arrange the "Crisper Basket" in the pot of Ninja Air Smart XL Indoor Grill.
3. Close the Ninja Air Smart XL Indoor Grill with lid and select "Air Crisp".
4. Set the temperature to 390 degrees F to preheat.
5. Press "Start/Stop" to begin preheating.

6. When the display shows "Add Food" open the lid and place the potatoes into the "Crisper Basket".
7. Close the Ninja Air Smart XL Indoor Grill with lid and set the time for 20 minutes.
8. Press "Start/Stop" to begin cooking.
9. Coat the potatoes twice with the remaining oil.
10. Meanwhile, in a frying pan, melt the butter over medium heat and sauté the onion for about 4-5 minutes.
11. Remove from the heat and transfer the onion into a bowl.
12. In the bowl of onion, add the potato flesh, chives, and half of cheese and stir to combine.
13. When the cooking time is completed, press "Start/Stop" to stop cooking.
14. Open the lid and transfer the potatoes onto a platter.
15. Carefully, cut each potato in half.
16. With a small scooper, scoop out the flesh from each half.
17. Stuff the potato halves with potato mixture evenly and sprinkle with the remaining cheese.
18. Again, arrange the potato halves in the "Crisper Basket".
19. Close the Ninja Air Smart XL Indoor Grill with lid and select "Air Crisp".
20. Set the temperature to 390 degrees F for 6 minutes.
21. Press "Start/Stop" to begin cooking.
22. When the cooking time is completed, press "Start/Stop" to stop cooking.
23. Open the lid and serve immediately.

Nutritional Information per Serving:

- Calories 276
- Total Fat 12.5 g
- Saturated Fat 3.6 g
- Cholesterol 16 mg
- Sodium 120 mg
- Total Carbs 34.8 g
- Fiber 5.4 g
- Sugar 3.1 g
- Protein 7.8 g

Stuffed Bell Peppers

Preparation Time: 15 minutes
Cooking Time: 15 minutes
Servings: 5

Ingredients:

- ½ of small bell pepper, seeded and chopped
- 1 (15-ounce) can diced tomatoes with juice
- 1 (15-ounce) can red kidney beans, rinsed and drained
- 1 cup cooked rice
- 1½ teaspoons Italian seasoning
- 5 large bell peppers, tops removed and seeded
- ½ cup mozzarella cheese, shredded
- 1 tablespoon Parmesan cheese, grated

Method:

1. In a bowl, mix together the chopped bell pepper, tomatoes with juice, beans, rice, and Italian seasoning.
2. Stuff each bell pepper with the rice mixture.
3. Arrange the greased "Crisper Basket" in the pot of Ninja Air Smart XL Indoor Grill.
4. Close the Ninja Air Smart XL Indoor Grill with lid and select "Air Crisp".
5. Set the temperature to 360 degrees F to preheat.
6. Press "Start/Stop" to begin preheating.
7. When the display shows "Add Food" open the lid and place the bell peppers into the "Crisper Basket".
8. Close the Ninja Air Smart XL Indoor Grill with lid and set the time for 15 minutes.
9. Press "Start/Stop" to begin cooking.
10. Meanwhile, in a bowl, mix together the mozzarella and Parmesan cheese.
11. After 12 minutes of cooking, top each bell pepper with cheese mixture.
12. When the cooking time is completed, press "Start/Stop" to stop cooking.
13. Open the lid and transfer the bell peppers onto a serving platter.
14. Serve warm.

Nutritional Information per Serving:

- Calories 404
- Total Fat 3.4 g
- Saturated Fat 13.4 g
- Cholesterol 183 mg
- Sodium 331 mg
- Total Carbs 2.1 g
- Fiber 0.7 g
- Sugar 10.2 g
- Protein 23.9 g

Glazed Veggies

Preparation Time: 15 minutes
Cooking Time: 25 minutes
Servings: 4
Ingredients:

- 2 ounces cherry tomatoes
- 2 large zucchini, chopped
- 2 green bell peppers, seeded and chopped
- 6 tablespoons olive oil, divided
- 2 tablespoons honey
- 1 teaspoon Dijon mustard
- 1 teaspoon dried herbs
- 1 teaspoon garlic paste
- Salt, as required

Method:

1. In a parchment paper-lined baking pan, place the vegetables and drizzle with 3 tablespoons of oil.
2. Arrange the "Crisper Basket" in the pot of Ninja Air Smart XL Indoor Grill.
3. Close the Ninja Air Smart XL Indoor Grill with lid and select "Air Crisp".
4. Set the temperature to 350 degrees F to preheat.
5. Press "Start/Stop" to begin preheating.
6. When the display shows "Add Food" open the lid and place the pan into the "Crisper Basket".
7. Close the Ninja Air Smart XL Indoor Grill with lid and set the time for 20 minutes.
8. Press "Start/Stop" to begin cooking.
9. Meanwhile, in a bowl, add the remaining oil, honey, mustard, herbs, garlic, salt, and black pepper and mix well.
10. When the cooking time is completed, press "Start/Stop" to stop cooking.
11. Open the lid and stir the honey mixture with vegetable mixture.
12. Again, arrange the pan into the "Crisper Basket".
13. Close the Ninja Air Smart XL Indoor Grill with lid and select "Air Crisp".
14. Set the temperature to 392 degrees F for 5 minutes.
15. Press "Start/Stop" to begin cooking.
16. When the cooking time is completed, press "Start/Stop" to stop cooking.
17. Open the lid and serve immediately.

Nutritional Information per Serving:

- Calories 262
- Total Fat 21.5 g
- Saturated Fat 3.1 g
- Cholesterol 0 mg
- Sodium 72 mg

- Total Carbs 19.5 g
- Fiber 2.9 g
- Sugar 14.8 g
- Protein 2.8 g

Veggie Ratatouille

Preparation Time: 15 minutes
Cooking Time: 15 minutes
Servings: 4
Ingredients:

- 1 green bell pepper, seeded and chopped
- 1 yellow bell pepper, seeded and chopped
- 1 eggplant, chopped
- 1 zucchini, chopped
- 3 tomatoes, chopped

- 2 small onions, chopped
- 2 garlic cloves, minced
- 2 tablespoons Herbs de Provence
- 1 tablespoon olive oil
- 1 tablespoon balsamic vinegar
- Salt and ground black pepper, as required

Method:

1. In a large bowl, add the vegetables, garlic, Herbs de Provence, oil, vinegar, salt, and black pepper and toss to coat well.
2. Transfer vegetable mixture into a greased baking pan.
3. Arrange the "Crisper Basket" in the pot of Ninja Air Smart XL Indoor Grill.
4. Close the Ninja Air Smart XL Indoor Grill with lid and select "Air Crisp".
5. Set the temperature to 355 degrees F to preheat.
6. Press "Start/Stop" to begin preheating.
7. When the display shows "Add Food" open the lid and place the pan into the "Crisper Basket".
8. Close the Ninja Air Smart XL Indoor Grill with lid and set the time for 15 minutes.
9. Press "Start/Stop" to begin cooking.
10. When the cooking time is completed, press "Start/Stop" to stop cooking.
11. Open the lid and serve hot.

Nutritional Information per Serving:

- Calories 119
- Total Fat 4.2 g
- Saturated Fat 0.6 g
- Cholesterol 0 mg
- Sodium 54 mg

- Total Carbs 20.3 g
- Fiber 7.3 g
- Sugar 11.2 g
- Protein 3.6 g

Marinated Tofu

Preparation Time: 15 minutes
Cooking Time: 20 minutes
Servings: 4
Ingredients:

- 2 tablespoons low-sodium soy sauce
- 2 tablespoon fish sauce
- 1 teaspoon sesame oil

- 12 ounces extra-firm tofu, drained and cubed into 1-inch size
- 1 teaspoon unsalted butter, melted

Method:

1. In a large bowl, place the soy sauce, fish sauce and sesame oil and mix until well combined.
2. Add the tofu cubes and toss to coat well.
3. Set aside to marinate for about 30 minutes, tossing occasionally.
4. Arrange the "Crisper Basket" in the pot of Ninja Air Smart XL Indoor Grill.
5. Close the Ninja Air Smart XL Indoor Grill with lid and select "Air Crisp".
6. Set the temperature to 355 degrees F to preheat.
7. Press "Start/Stop" to begin preheating.
8. When the display shows "Add Food" open the lid and place the tofu cubes into the "Crisper Basket".
9. Drizzle the tofu cubes with the melted butter.
10. Close the Ninja Air Smart XL Indoor Grill with lid and set the time for 25 minutes.
11. Press "Start/Stop" to begin cooking.
12. After 13 minutes of cooking, flip the tofu cubes.
13. When the cooking time is completed, press "Start/Stop" to stop cooking.
14. Open the lid and serve hot.

Nutritional Information per Serving:

- Calories 102

- Total Fat 7.1 g

- Saturated Fat 1.2 g
- Cholesterol 3 mg
- Sodium 1100 mg
- Total Carbs 2.5 g
- Fiber 0.3 g
- Sugar 1.3 g
- Protein 9.4 g

Tofu with Orange Sauce

Preparation Time: 10 minutes
Cooking Time: 20 minutes
Servings: 4
Ingredients:
For Tofu

- 1 pound extra-firm tofu, pressed and cubed

For Sauce

- ½ cup water
- 1/3 cup fresh orange juice
- 1 tablespoon honey
- 1 teaspoon orange zest, grated
- 1 teaspoon garlic, minced
- 1 tablespoon cornstarch
- 1 tablespoon tamari

- 1 teaspoon fresh ginger, minced
- 2 teaspoons cornstarch
- ¼ teaspoon red pepper flakes, crushed

Method:

1. In a bowl, add the tofu, cornstarch, and tamari and toss to coat well.
2. Set the tofu aside to marinate for at least 15 minutes.
3. Arrange the greased "Crisper Basket" in the pot of Ninja Air Smart XL Indoor Grill.
4. Close the Ninja Air Smart XL Indoor Grill with lid and select "Air Crisp".
5. Set the temperature to 390 degrees F to preheat.
6. Press "Start/Stop" to begin preheating.
7. When the display shows "Add Food" open the lid and place the tofu cubes into the "Crisper Basket".
8. Close the Ninja Air Smart XL Indoor Grill with lid and set the time for 10 minutes.
9. Press "Start/Stop" to begin cooking.
10. Meanwhile, for the sauce: in a small pan, add all the ingredients over medium-high heat and bring to a boil, stirring continuously.

11. When the cooking time is completed, press "Start/Stop" to stop cooking.

12. Open the lid and transfer the tofu into a serving bowl.

13. Add the sauce and gently stir to combine.

14. Serve immediately.

Nutritional Information per Serving:

- Calories 147
- Total Fat 6.7 g
- Saturated Fat 0.6 g
- Cholesterol 0 mg
- Sodium 262 mg
- Total Carbs 12.7 g
- Fiber 0.7 g
- Sugar 6.7 g
- Protein 12.1 g

Chapter 8: Appetizer & Snacks Recipes

Buffalo Chicken Wings

Preparation Time: 150 minutes
Cooking Time: 16 minutes
Servings: 5
Ingredients:

- 2 pounds frozen chicken wings, drums and flats separated
- 2 tablespoons olive oil
- 2 tablespoons Buffalo sauce
- ½ teaspoon red pepper flakes, crushed
- Salt, as required

Method:

1. Coat the chicken wings with oi evenly.
2. Arrange the "Crisper Basket" in the pot of Ninja Air Smart XL Indoor Grill.
3. Close the Ninja Air Smart XL Indoor Grill with lid and select "Air Crisp".
4. Set the temperature to 390 degrees F to preheat.
5. Press "Start/Stop" to begin preheating.
6. When the display shows "Add Food" open the lid and place the chicken wings into the "Crisper Basket".
7. Close the Ninja Air Smart XL Indoor Grill with lid and set the time for 16 minutes.
8. Press "Start/Stop" to begin cooking.
9. After 12 minutes of cooking, flip the wings and coat with barbecue sauce evenly.
10. Meanwhile, in a large bowl, add Buffalo sauce, red pepper flakes and salt and mix well.
11. When the cooking time is completed, press "Start/Stop" to stop cooking.
12. Open the lid and transfer the wings into a bowl.
13. Add the Buffalo sauce and toss to coat well.
14. Serve immediately.

Nutritional Information per Serving:

- Calories 394
- Total Fat 19.1 g
- Saturated Fat 4.5 g
- Cholesterol 161 mg
- Sodium 339mg
- Total Carbs 0.2 g

- Fiber 0.1g
- Sugar 0.1 g

- Protein 52.5 g

BBQ Chicken Wings

Preparation Time: 15 minutes
Cooking Time: 19 minutes
Servings: 4
Ingredients:

- 2 pounds chicken wings
- 1 teaspoon olive oil
- 1 teaspoon smoked paprika
- 1 teaspoon garlic powder

- Salt and ground black pepper, as required
- ¼ cup barbecue sauce

Method:

1. In a large bowl combine chicken wings, smoked paprika, garlic powder, oil, salt, and pepper and mix well.
2. Arrange the "Crisper Basket" in the pot of Ninja Air Smart XL Indoor Grill.
3. Close the Ninja Air Smart XL Indoor Grill with lid and select "Air Crisp".
4. Set the temperature to 360 degrees F to preheat.
5. Press "Start/Stop" to begin preheating.
6. When the display shows "Add Food" open the lid and place the chicken wings the "Crisper Basket" in a single layer.
7. Close the Ninja Air Smart XL Indoor Grill with lid and select "Air Crisp".
8. Set the temperature to 360 degrees F for 19 minutes.
9. Press "Start/Stop" to begin cooking.
10. After 12 minutes of cooking, flip the wings and coat with barbecue sauce evenly.
11. When the cooking time is completed, press "Start/Stop" to stop cooking.
12. Open the lid and serve immediately.

Nutritional Information per Serving:

- Calories 468
- Total Fat 18.1 g
- Saturated Fat 4.8 g
- Cholesterol 202 mg
- Sodium 409 mg

- Total Carbs 6.5 g
- Fiber 0.4 g
- Sugar 4.3 g
- Protein 65.8 g

Crispy Chicken Wings

Preparation Time: 15 minutes
Cooking Time: 25 minutes
Servings: 3
Ingredients:

- 1 onion, finely chopped
- 1 teaspoon lemon zest, grated
- 1 tablespoon soy sauce
- 1½ tablespoons honey
- Ground white pepper, as required
- 1 pound chicken wings, rinsed and trimmed
- ½ cup cornstarch

Method:

1. In a bowl, mix together the lemongrass, onion, soy sauce, honey, salt, and white pepper.
2. Add the wings and coat with marinade generously.
3. Cover and refrigerate to marinate overnight.
4. Arrange the greased "Crisper Basket" in the pot of Ninja Air Smart XL Indoor Grill.
5. Close the Ninja Air Smart XL Indoor Grill with lid and select "Air Crisp".
6. Set the temperature to 355 degrees F to preheat.
7. Press "Start/Stop" to begin preheating.
8. Remove the chicken wings from marinade and coat with the cornstarch.
9. When the display shows "Add Food" open the lid and place the chicken wings the "Crisper Basket" in a single layer.
10. Close the Ninja Air Smart XL Indoor Grill with lid and select "Air Crisp".
11. Set the temperature to 360 degrees F for 25 minutes.
12. Press "Start/Stop" to begin cooking.
13. After 13 minutes of cooking, flip the wings once.
14. When the cooking time is completed, press "Start/Stop" to stop cooking.
15. Open the lid and serve hot.

Nutritional Information per Serving:

- Calories 418
- Total Fat 11.3 g
- Saturated Fat 3.1 g
- Cholesterol 135 mg
- Sodium 434 mg
- Total Carbs 32.1 g
- Fiber 1.1 g
- Sugar 10.3 g

- Protein 44.6 g

Bacon-Wrapped Shrimp

Preparation Time: 15 minutes
Cooking Time: 7 minutes
Servings: 6
Ingredients:

- 1 pound bacon, thinly sliced
- 1 pound shrimp, peeled and deveined

Method:

1. Wrap each shrimp with one bacon slice.
2. Arrange the shrimp in a baking dish and refrigerate for about 20 minutes.
3. Arrange the "Crisper Basket" in the pot of Ninja Air Smart XL Indoor Grill.
4. Close the Ninja Air Smart XL Indoor Grill with lid and select "Air Crisp".
5. Set the temperature to 390 degrees F to preheat.
6. Press "Start/Stop" to begin preheating.
7. When the display shows "Add Food" open the lid and place the shrimp in the "Crisper Basket" in a single layer.
8. Close the Ninja Air Smart XL Indoor Grill with lid and set the time for 7 minutes.
9. Press "Start/Stop" to begin cooking.
10. When the cooking time is completed, press "Start/Stop" to stop cooking.
11. Open the lid and serve warm.

Nutritional Information per Serving:

- Calories 499
- Total Fat 32.9 g
- Saturated Fat 10.8 g
- Cholesterol 242 mg
- Sodium 1930 mg
- Total Carbs 2.2 g
- Fiber 0 g
- Sugar 0 g
- Protein 42.5 g

Crispy Shrimp

Preparation Time: 20 minutes
Cooking Time: 20 minutes
Servings: 4
Ingredients:

- 8 ounces coconut milk
- Salt and ground black pepper, as required
- ½ cup panko breadcrumbs
- ½ teaspoon cayenne pepper
- 1 pound shrimp, peeled and deveined

Method:

1. In a shallow dish, mix together the coconut milk, salt and black pepper.
2. In another shallow dish, mix together breadcrumbs, cayenne pepper, salt and black pepper.
3. Dip the shrimp in coconut milk mixture and then coat with the breadcrumbs mixture.
4. Arrange the "Crisper Basket" in the pot of Ninja Air Smart XL Indoor Grill.
5. Close the Ninja Air Smart XL Indoor Grill with lid and select "Air Crisp".
6. Set the temperature to 350 degrees F to preheat.
7. Press "Start/Stop" to begin preheating.
8. When the display shows "Add Food" open the lid and place the shrimp into the "Crisper Basket".
9. Close the Ninja Air Smart XL Indoor Grill with lid and set the time for 20 minutes.
10. Press "Start/Stop" to begin cooking.
11. When the cooking time is completed, press "Start/Stop" to stop cooking.
12. Open the lid and serve warm.

Nutritional Information per Serving:

- Calories 301
- Total Fat 15.7 g
- Saturated Fat 12.6 g
- Cholesterol 239 mg
- Sodium 393 mg
- Total Carbs 12.5 g
- Fiber 2.3 g
- Sugar 2.2 g
- Protein 28.2 g

Creamy Breaded Shrimp

Preparation Time: 15 minutes
Cooking Time: 20 minutes
Servings: 4
Ingredients:

- ¼ cup all-purpose flour
- ½ cup mayonnaise
- ¼ cup sweet chili sauce
- 1 tablespoon Sriracha sauce

- 1 cup panko breadcrumbs
- 1 pound shrimp, peeled and deveined

Method:

1. In a shallow bowl, place the flour.
2. In a second bowl, mix together the mayonnaise, chili sauce, and Sriracha sauce.
3. In a third bowl, add the breadcrumbs.
4. Coat each shrimp with the flour, then dip into mayonnaise mixture and finally, coat with the breadcrumbs.
5. Arrange the greased "Crisper Basket" in the pot of Ninja Air Smart XL Indoor Grill.
6. Close the Ninja Air Smart XL Indoor Grill with lid and select "Air Crisp".
7. Set the temperature to 400 degrees F to preheat.
8. Press "Start/Stop" to begin preheating.
9. When the display shows "Add Food" open the lid and place half of the shrimp into the "Crisper Basket".
10. Close the Ninja Air Smart XL Indoor Grill with lid and set the time for 10 minutes.
11. Press "Start/Stop" to begin cooking.
12. When the cooking time is completed, press "Start/Stop" to stop cooking.
13. Open the lid and transfer the shrimp onto a platter.
14. Repeat with the remaining shrimp.
15. Serve hot.

Nutritional Information per Serving:

- Calories 402
- Total Fat 16.2 g
- Saturated Fat 3.2 g
- Cholesterol 249 mg
- Sodium 895 mg
- Total Carbs 19.3 g
- Fiber 0.4 g
- Sugar 2.4 g
- Protein 27.7 g

Bread Rolls

Preparation Time: 20 minutes
Cooking Time: 33 minutes
Servings: 8
Ingredients:

- 5 large potatoes, peeled
- 2 tablespoons vegetable oil, divided

- 2 small onions, finely chopped
- 2 green chilies, seeded and chopped
- 2 curry leaves
- ½ teaspoon ground turmeric
- Salt, as required
- 8 bread slices, trimmed

Method:

1. In a pan of the boiling water, add the potatoes and cook for about 15-20 minutes.
2. Drain the potatoes well and with a potato masher, mash the potatoes.
3. In a skillet, heat 1 teaspoon of oil over a medium heat and sauté the onion for about 4-5 minutes.
4. Add the green chilies, curry leaves, and turmeric and sauté for about 1 minute.
5. Add in the mashed potatoes, and salt and mix well.
6. Remove from the heat and set aside to cool completely.
7. Make 8 equal-sized oval-shaped patties from the mixture.
8. Wet the bread slices completely with water.
9. With your hands, press each bread slices to remove the excess water.
10. Place 1 bread slice in your palm and place 1 patty in the center.
11. Roll the bread slice in a spindle shape and seal the edges to secure the filling.
12. Coat the roll with some oil.
13. Repeat with the remaining slices, filling and oil.
14. Arrange the "Crisper Basket" in the pot of Ninja Air Smart XL Indoor Grill.
15. Close the Ninja Air Smart XL Indoor Grill with lid and select "Air Crisp".
16. Set the temperature to 390 degrees F to preheat.
17. Press "Start/Stop" to begin preheating.
18. When the display shows "Add Food" open the lid and place the rolls into the "Crisper Basket".
19. Close the Ninja Air Smart XL Indoor Grill with lid and set the time for 13 minutes.
20. Press "Start/Stop" to begin cooking.
21. When the cooking time is completed, press "Start/Stop" to stop cooking.
22. Open the lid and serve warm.

Nutritional Information per Serving:

- Calories 221
- Total Fat 4 g
- Saturated Fat 0.8 g
- Cholesterol 0 mg
- Sodium 95 mg
- Total Carbs 42.6 g
- Fiber 6.2 g
- Sugar 3.8 g

- Protein 4.8 g

Broccoli Bites

Preparation Time: 20 minutes
Cooking Time: 12 minutes
Servings: 6
Ingredients:

- 2 cups broccoli florets
- 2 eggs, beaten
- 1¼ cups cheddar cheese, grated
- ¼ cup Parmesan cheese, grated
- 1¼ cups panko breadcrumbs
- Salt and ground black pepper, as required

Method:

1. In a food processor, add the broccoli and pulse until crumbed finely.
2. In a large bowl, place the broccoli and remaining ingredients and mix until well combined.
3. Make small equal-sized balls from mixture.
4. Arrange the balls onto a parchment-lined baking sheet and refrigerate for at least 30 minutes.
5. Arrange the "Crisper Basket" in the pot of Ninja Air Smart XL Indoor Grill.
6. Close the Ninja Air Smart XL Indoor Grill with lid and select "Air Crisp".
7. Set the temperature to 350 degrees F to preheat.
8. Press "Start/Stop" to begin preheating.
9. When the display shows "Add Food" open the lid and place the broccoli balls into the "Crisper Basket" in a single layer.
10. Close the Ninja Air Smart XL Indoor Grill with lid and set the time for 12 minutes.
11. Press "Start/Stop" to begin cooking.
12. When the cooking time is completed, press "Start/Stop" to stop cooking.
13. Open the lid and serve warm.

Nutritional Information per Serving:

- Calories 247
- Total Fat 13.6 g
- Saturated Fat 7.7 g
- Cholesterol 83 mg
- Sodium 457 mg
- Total Carbs 6.5 g
- Fiber 0.9 g
- Sugar 0.8 g

- Protein 13.2 g

Chicken Nuggets

Preparation Time: 20 minutes
Cooking Time: 10 minutes
Servings: 5
Ingredients:

- ½ of zucchini, chopped roughly
- ½ of carrot, peeled and chopped roughly
- 14 ounces boneless, skinless chicken breasts, cut into chunks
- ½ tablespoon mustard powder
- 1 tablespoon garlic powder
- 1 tablespoon onion powder
- Salt and ground black pepper, as required
- 1 cup all-purpose flour
- 2 tablespoons milk
- 1 egg
- 1 cup panko breadcrumbs

Method:

1. In a food processor, add zucchini and carrot and pulse until chopped finely.
2. Add the chicken, mustard powder, garlic powder, onion powder, salt and black pepper and pulse until just combined.
3. Make equal-sized nuggets from the mixture.
4. In a shallow dish, place the flour.
5. In a second shallow dish, beat the milk and egg.
6. In a third shallow dish, place the breadcrumbs.
7. Coat the nuggets with flour, then dip into egg mixture and finally, coat with the breadcrumbs.
8. Arrange the "Crisper Basket" in the pot of Ninja Air Smart XL Indoor Grill.
9. Close the Ninja Air Smart XL Indoor Grill with lid and select "Air Crisp".
10. Set the temperature to 390 degrees F to preheat.
11. Press "Start/Stop" to begin preheating.
12. When the display shows "Add Food" open the lid and place the nuggets into the "Crisper Basket" in a single layer.
13. Close the Ninja Air Smart XL Indoor Grill with lid and set the time for 10 minutes.
14. Press "Start/Stop" to begin cooking.
15. When the cooking time is completed, press "Start/Stop" to stop cooking.

16. Open the lid and serve warm.

Nutritional Information per Serving:

- Calories 357
- Total Fat 9 g
- Saturated Fat 2.6 g
- Cholesterol 104 mg
- Sodium 122 mg
- Total Carbs 26.7 g
- Fiber 1.5 g
- Sugar 2.1 g
- Protein 28.4 g

Potato Croquettes

Preparation Time: 15 minutes

Cooking Time: 23 minutes

Servings: 4

Ingredients:

- 2 medium Russet potatoes, peeled and cubed
- 2 tablespoons all-purpose flour
- ½ cup Parmesan cheese, grated
- 1 egg yolk
- 2 tablespoons chives, minced
- Pinch of ground nutmeg
- Salt and ground black pepper, as required
- 2 eggs
- ½ cup breadcrumbs
- 2 tablespoons vegetable oil

Method:

1. In a pan of boiling water, add potatoes and cook for about 15 minutes.
2. Drain the potatoes well and transfer into a large bowl.
3. With a potato masher, mash the potatoes and set aside to cool completely.
4. In the same bowl of mashed potatoes, add in the flour, Parmesan cheese, egg yolk, chives, nutmeg, salt, and black pepper and mix until well combined.
5. Make small equal-sized balls from the mixture.
6. Now, roll each ball into a cylinder shape.
7. In a shallow dish, crack the eggs and beat well.
8. In another dish, mix together the breadcrumbs and oil.
9. Dip the croquettes in egg mixture and then coat with the breadcrumbs mixture.
10. Arrange the "Crisper Basket" in the pot of Ninja Air Smart XL Indoor Grill.
11. Close the Ninja Air Smart XL Indoor Grill with lid and select "Air Crisp".
12. Set the temperature to 390 degrees F to preheat.
13. Press "Start/Stop" to begin preheating.

14. When the display shows "Add Food" open the lid and place the croquettes into the "Crisper Basket" in a single layer.
15. Close the Ninja Air Smart XL Indoor Grill with lid and set the time for 8 minutes.
16. Press "Start/Stop" to begin cooking.
17. When the cooking time is completed, press "Start/Stop" to stop cooking.
18. Open the lid and serve warm.

Nutritional Information per Serving:

- Calories 283
- Total Fat 13.4 g
- Saturated Fat 3.8 g
- Cholesterol 142 mg
- Sodium 263 mg
- Total Carbs 29.9 g
- Fiber 3.3 g
- Sugar 2.3 g
- Protein 11.5 g

Bacon Croquettes

Preparation Time: 20 minutes
Cooking Time: 8 minutes
Servings: 8
Ingredients:

- 1 pound thin bacon slices
- 1 pound sharp cheddar cheese block, cut into 1-inch rectangular pieces
- 1 cup all-purpose flour
- 3 eggs
- 1 cup breadcrumbs
- Salt, as required
- ¼ cup olive oil

Method:
1. Wrap 2 bacon slices around 1 piece of cheddar cheese, covering completely.
2. Repeat with the remaining bacon and cheese pieces.
3. Arrange the croquettes in a baking dish and freeze for about 5 minutes.
4. In a shallow dish, place the flour.
5. In a second shallow dish, crack the eggs and beat well.
6. In a third shallow dish, mix together the breadcrumbs, salt, and oil.
7. Coat the croquettes with flour, then dip into beaten eggs and finally coat with the breadcrumbs mixture.
8. Arrange the "Crisper Basket" in the pot of Ninja Air Smart XL Indoor Grill.
9. Close the Ninja Air Smart XL Indoor Grill with lid and select "Air Crisp".
10. Set the temperature to 390 degrees F to preheat.

11. Press "Start/Stop" to begin preheating.
12. When the display shows "Add Food" open the lid and place the croquettes into the "Crisper Basket" in a single layer.
13. Close the Ninja Air Smart XL Indoor Grill with lid and set the time for 8 minutes.
14. Press "Start/Stop" to begin cooking.
15. When the cooking time is completed, press "Start/Stop" to stop cooking.
16. Open the lid and serve warm.

Nutritional Information per Serving:

- Calories 591
- Total Fat 43.5 g
- Saturated Fat 13.8 g
- Cholesterol 143 mg
- Total Carbs 23.4 g
- Sodium 1600 mg
- Fiber 1.6 g
- Sugar 1.3 g
- Protein 26.6 g

Mozzarella Sticks

Preparation Time: 15 minutes
Cooking Time: 12 minutes
Servings: 3
Ingredients:

- 3 tablespoons white flour
- 2 eggs
- 3 tablespoons milk
- ½ cup plain breadcrumbs
- ½ pound mozzarella cheese block, cut into 3x½-inch sticks

Method:

1. In a shallow dish, place the flour.
2. In a second shallow dish, add eggs and milk and beat well.
3. In a third shallow dish, place the breadcrumbs.
4. Coat the Mozzarella sticks with flour, then dip into egg mixture and finally, coat with the breadcrumbs.
5. Arrange the Mozzarella sticks onto a cookie sheet and freeze for about 1-2 hours.
6. Arrange the "Crisper Basket" in the pot of Ninja Air Smart XL Indoor Grill.
7. Close the Ninja Air Smart XL Indoor Grill with lid and select "Air Crisp".
8. Set the temperature to 400 degrees F to preheat.
9. Press "Start/Stop" to begin preheating.

10. When the display shows "Add Food" open the lid and place the mozzarella sticks into the "Crisper Basket".

11. Close the Ninja Air Smart XL Indoor Grill with lid and set the time for 12 minutes.

12. Press "Start/Stop" to begin cooking.

13. When the cooking time is completed, press "Start/Stop" to stop cooking.

14. Open the lid and serve warm.

Nutritional Information per Serving:

- Calories 162
- Total Fat 5.1 g
- Saturated Fat 1.8 g
- Cholesterol 113 mg
- Sodium 209 mg
- Total Carbs 20.1 g
- Fiber 1 g
- Sugar 2.1 g
- Protein 8.7 g

French Fries

Preparation Time: 15 minutes
Cooking Time: 30 minutes
Servings: 4
Ingredients:

- 1 pound potatoes, peeled and cut into strips
- 3 tablespoons olive oil
- ½ teaspoon onion powder
- ½ teaspoon garlic powder
- 1 teaspoon paprika

Method:

1. In a large bowl of water, soak the potato strips for about 1 hour.
2. Drain the potato strips well and pat them dry with the paper towels.
3. In a large bowl, add the potato strips and the remaining ingredients and toss to coat well.
4. Arrange the "Crisper Basket" in the pot of Ninja Air Smart XL Indoor Grill.
5. Close the Ninja Air Smart XL Indoor Grill with lid and select "Air Crisp".
6. Set the temperature to 375 degrees F to preheat.
7. Press "Start/Stop" to begin preheating.
8. When the display shows "Add Food" open the lid and place the potato fries into the "Crisper Basket".

9. Close the Ninja Air Smart XL Indoor Grill with lid and set the time for 30 minutes.
10. Press "Start/Stop" to begin cooking.
11. When the cooking time is completed, press "Start/Stop" to stop cooking.
12. Open the lid and serve warm.

Nutritional Information per Serving:

- Calories 172
- Total Fat 10.7 g
- Saturated Fat 1.5 g
- Cholesterol 0 mg
- Sodium 7 mg
- Total Carbs 18.6 g
- Fiber 3 g
- Sugar 1.6 g
- Protein 2.1 g

Zucchini Fries

Preparation Time: 10 minutes
Cooking Time: 20 minutes
Servings: 4
Ingredients:

- 1 pound zucchini, sliced into 2½-inch sticks
- Salt, as required
- 2 tablespoons olive oil
- ¾ cup panko breadcrumbs

Method:

1. In a colander, add the zucchini and sprinkle with salt. Set aside for about 10 minutes.
2. Gently pat dry the zucchini sticks with the paper towels and coat with oil.
3. In a shallow dish, add the breadcrumbs.
4. Coat the zucchini sticks with breadcrumbs evenly.
5. Arrange the "Crisper Basket" in the pot of Ninja Air Smart XL Indoor Grill.
6. Close the Ninja Air Smart XL Indoor Grill with lid and select "Air Crisp".
7. Set the temperature to 390 degrees F to preheat.
8. Press "Start/Stop" to begin preheating.
9. When the display shows "Add Food" open the lid and place half of the zucchini fries into the "Crisper Basket".
10. Close the Ninja Air Smart XL Indoor Grill with lid and set the temperature to 425 degrees F for 10 minutes.

11. Press "Start/Stop" to begin cooking.

12. When the cooking time is completed, press "Start/Stop" to stop cooking.

13. Open the lid and transfer the fries onto a platter.

14. Repeat with the remaining fries.

15. Serve warm.

Nutritional Information per Serving:

- Calories 78
- Total Fat 8.6 g
- Saturated Fat 1.6 g
- Cholesterol 0 mg
- Sodium 50 mg
- Total Carbs 6.9 g
- Fiber 1.3 g
- Sugar 2 g
- Protein.1.9 g

Apple Chips

Preparation Time: 15 minutes

Cooking Time: 8 minutes

Servings: 2

Ingredients:

- 1 apple, peeled, cored and sliced thinly
- 1 tablespoon sugar
- ½ teaspoon ground cinnamon
- Pinch of ground ginger
- Pinch of salt

Method:

1. In a bowl, place all ingredients and toss to coat well.

2. Arrange the "Crisper Basket" in the pot of Ninja Air Smart XL Indoor Grill.

3. Close the Ninja Air Smart XL Indoor Grill with lid and select "Air Crisp".

4. Set the temperature to 390 degrees F to preheat.

5. Press "Start/Stop" to begin preheating.

6. When the display shows "Add Food" open the lid and place the apple chips into the "Crisper Basket".

7. Close the Ninja Air Smart XL Indoor Grill with lid and set the time for 8 minutes.

8. Press "Start/Stop" to begin cooking.

9. After 4 minutes of cooking, flip the apple chips.

10. When the cooking time is completed, press "Start/Stop" to stop cooking.

11. Open the lid and transfer the apple chis onto a tray.

12. Set aside to cool before serving.

Nutritional Information per Serving:

- Calories 82
- Total Fat 0.2 g
- Saturated Fat 0 g
- Cholesterol 0 mg
- Total Carbs 22 g

- Sodium 79 mg
- Fiber 3 g
- Sugar 17.6 g
- Protein 0.3 g

Chapter 9: Dessert Recipes

Stuffed Apples

Preparation Time: 15 minutes
Cooking Time: 13 minutes
Servings: 4
Ingredients:
For Stuffed Apples

- 4 small firm apples, cored
- ½ cup golden raisins
- ½ cup blanched almonds
- 2 tablespoons sugar

For Vanilla Sauce

- ½ cup whipped cream
- 2 tablespoons sugar
- ½ teaspoon vanilla extract

Method:
1. In a food processor, add the raisins, almonds, and sugar and pulse until chopped.
2. Carefully, stuff each apple with raisin mixture.
3. Close the Ninja Air Smart XL Indoor Grill with lid and select "Air Crisp".
4. Set the temperature to 355 degrees F to preheat.
5. Press "Start/Stop" to begin preheating.
6. Line a baking pan with a parchment paper.
7. Place apples into the prepared baking pan.
8. When the display shows "Add Food" open the lid and place the baking pan into the Grill.
9. Close the Ninja Air Smart XL Indoor Grill with lid and set the time for 10 minutes.
10. Press "Start/Stop" to begin cooking.
11. Meanwhile, for vanilla sauce: in a pan, add the cream, sugar, and vanilla extract over medium heat and cook for about 2-3 minutes or until sugar is dissolved, stirring continuously.
12. When the cooking time is completed, press "Start/Stop" to stop cooking.
13. Open the lid and transfer the apples onto the serving plates.
14. Set aside to cool slightly
15. Top with the vanilla sauce and serve.

Nutritional Information per Serving:

- Calories 329
- Total Fat 11.1 g
- Saturated Fat 3.4 g
- Cholesterol 17 mg
- Sodium 9 mg
- Total Carbs 60.2 g
- Fiber 7.6 g
- Sugar 46.5 g
- Protein 4 g

Banana Split

Preparation Time: 15 minutes
Cooking Time: 14 minutes
Servings: 8
Ingredients:

- 3 tablespoons coconut oil
- 1 cup panko breadcrumbs
- ½ cup corn flour
- 2 eggs
- 4 bananas, peeled and halved lengthwise
- 3 tablespoons sugar
- ¼ teaspoon ground cinnamon
- 2 tablespoons walnuts, chopped

Method:

1. In a medium skillet, melt the coconut oil over medium heat and cook breadcrumbs for about 3-4 minutes or until golden browned and crumbled, stirring continuously.
2. Transfer the breadcrumbs into a shallow bowl and set aside to cool.
3. In a second bowl, place the corn flour.
4. In a third bowl, whisk the eggs.
5. Coat the banana slices with flour and then, dip into eggs and finally, coat evenly with the breadcrumbs.
6. In a small bowl, mix together the sugar and cinnamon.
7. Arrange the "Crisper Basket" in the pot of Ninja Air Smart XL Indoor Grill.
8. Close the Ninja Air Smart XL Indoor Grill with lid and select "Air Crisp".
9. Set the temperature to 280 degrees F to preheat.
10. Press "Start/Stop" to begin preheating.
11. When the display shows "Add Food" open the lid and place the banana slices into the "Crisper Basket".
12. Sprinkle the banana slices with cinnamon sugar.

13. Close the Ninja Air Smart XL Indoor Grill with lid and set the time for 10 minutes.
14. Press "Start/Stop" to begin cooking.
15. When the cooking time is completed, press "Start/Stop" to stop cooking.
16. Open the lid and transfer the banana slices onto serving plates.
17. Set aside to cool slightly
18. Sprinkle with chopped walnuts and serve.

Nutritional Information per Serving:

- Calories 216
- Total Fat 8.8g
- Saturated Fat 5.3 g
- Cholesterol 41 mg
- Sodium 16 mg
- Total Carbs 26 g
- Fiber 2.3 g
- Sugar 11.9 g
- Protein 3.4 g

Chocolate Muffins

Preparation Time: 15 minutes
Cooking Time: 15 minutes
Servings: 12
Ingredients:

- 1 1/3 cups self-rising flour
- 2/3 cup plus 3 tablespoons caster sugar
- 2½ tablespoons cocoa powder
- 3½ ounces butter
- 5 tablespoons milk
- 2 medium eggs
- ½ teaspoon vanilla extract
- Water, as required
- ½ ounce milk chocolate, finely chopped

Method:

1. In a bowl, mix well flour, sugar, and cocoa powder.
2. With a pastry cutter, cut in the butter until a breadcrumb like mixture forms.
3. In another bowl, mix together the milk, and eggs.
4. Add the egg mixture into flour mixture and mix until well combined.
5. Add the vanilla extract and a little water and mix until well combined.
6. Fold in the chopped chocolate.
7. Grease 12 muffin molds.
8. Transfer mixture evenly into the prepared muffin molds.

9. Arrange the "Crisper Basket" in the pot of Ninja Air Smart XL Indoor Grill.
10. Close the Ninja Air Smart XL Indoor Grill with lid and select "Air Crisp".
11. Set the temperature to 355 degrees F to preheat.
12. Press "Start/Stop" to begin preheating.
13. When the display shows "Add Food" open the lid and place the muffin molds into the "Crisper Basket".
14. Close the Ninja Air Smart XL Indoor Grill with lid and set the time for 9 minutes.
15. Press "Start/Stop" to begin cooking.
16. After 9 minutes of cooking, set the temperature to 320 degrees F for 6 minutes.
17. When the cooking time is completed, press "Start/Stop" to stop cooking.
18. Open the lid and place the muffin molds onto a wire rack to cool for about 10 minutes.
19. Now, invert the muffins onto the wire rack to cool completely before serving.

Nutritional Information per Serving:

- Calories 389
- Total Fat 31.2 g
- Saturated Fat 19.5 g
- Cholesterol 107 mg
- Sodium 226 mg
- Total Carbs 26.3 g
- Fiber 0.8 g
- Sugar 15.1 g
- Protein 3.2 g

Lava Cake

Preparation Time: 15 minutes
Cooking Time: 12½ minutes
Servings: 4

Ingredients:

- 2/3 cup chocolate chips
- ½ cup unsalted butter
- 2 large eggs
- 2 large egg yolks
- 1 cup confectioners' sugar
- 1 teaspoon peppermint extract
- 1/3 cup all-purpose flour plus more for dusting
- 2 tablespoons powdered sugar
- ¼ cup fresh raspberries

Method:

1. In a microwave-safe bowl, place the chocolate chips and butter and microwave on High for about 30 seconds.
2. Remove the bowl from microwave and stir the mixture well.

3. Add the eggs, egg yolks and confectioners' sugar and beat until well combined.
4. Add the flour and gently, stir to combine.
5. Grease 4 ramekins and dust each with a little flour.
6. Place the chocolate mixture into the prepared ramekins evenly.
7. Arrange the "Crisper Basket" in the pot of Ninja Air Smart XL Indoor Grill.
8. Close the Ninja Air Smart XL Indoor Grill with lid and select "Air Crisp".
9. Set the temperature to 375 degrees F to preheat.
10. Press "Start/Stop" to begin preheating.
11. When the display shows "Add Food" open the lid and place the ramekins into the "Crisper Basket".
12. Close the Ninja Air Smart XL Indoor Grill with lid and set the time for 12 minutes.
13. Press "Start/Stop" to begin cooking.
14. When the cooking time is completed, press "Start/Stop" to stop cooking.
15. Open the lid and transfer the ramekins onto a wire rack for about 5 minutes.
16. Carefully run a knife around the sides of each ramekin many times to loosen the cake.
17. Carefully, invert each cake onto a dessert plate and dust with powdered sugar.
18. Garnish with raspberries and serve immediately.

Nutritional Information per Serving:

- Calories 596
- Total Fat 36.2 g
- Saturated Fat 22 g
- Cholesterol 265 mg
- Sodium 225 mg
- Total Carbs 60.1 g
- Fiber 1.7 g
- Sugar 19.1 g
- Protein 8.1 g

Banana Mug Cake

Preparation Time: 10 minutes
Cooking Time: 30 minutes
Servings: 1
Ingredients:

- ¼ cup all-purpose flour
- 1/8 teaspoon ground cinnamon
- ¼ teaspoon baking soda
- 1/8 teaspoon salt
- ½ cup banana, peeled and mashed
- 2 tablespoons sugar

- 1 tablespoon butter, melted
- 1 egg yolk
- ¼ teaspoon vanilla extract

Method:

1. In a bowl, mix together the flour, baking soda, cinnamon and salt.
2. In another bowl, add the mashed banana and sugar and beat well.
3. Add the butter, the egg yolk, and the vanilla and mix well.
4. Add the flour mixture and mix until just combined.
5. Place the mixture into a lightly greased ramekin.
6. Arrange the "Crisper Basket" in the pot of Ninja Air Smart XL Indoor Grill.
7. Close the Ninja Air Smart XL Indoor Grill with lid and select "Bake".
8. Set the temperature to 350 degrees F to preheat.
9. Press "Start/Stop" to begin preheating.
10. When the display shows "Add Food" open the lid and place the ramekin into the "Crisper Basket".
11. Close the Ninja Air Smart XL Indoor Grill with lid and set the time for 30 minutes.
12. Press "Start/Stop" to begin cooking.
13. When the cooking time is completed, press "Start/Stop" to stop cooking.
14. Open the lid and place the ramekin onto a wire rack to cool slightly before serving.

Nutritional Information per Serving:

- Calories 430
- Total Fat 16.6 g
- Saturated Fat 9 g
- Cholesterol 240 mg
- Sodium 697 mg
- Total Carbs 66 g
- Fiber 2.9 g
- Sugar 33.5 g
- Protein 6.9 g

Chocolate Brownie Cake

Preparation Time: 15 minutes
Cooking Time: 35 minutes
Servings: 6
Ingredients:

- ½ cup dark chocolate chips
- ½ cup butter
- 3 eggs
- ¼ cup sugar
- 1 teaspoon vanilla extract

Method:

1. In a microwave-safe bowl, add the chocolate chips and butter and microwave for about 1 minute, stirring after every 20 seconds.
2. Remove from the microwave and stir well.
3. Arrange the "Crisper Basket" in the pot of Ninja Air Smart XL Indoor Grill.
4. Close the Ninja Air Smart XL Indoor Grill with lid and select "Air Crisp".
5. Set the temperature to 350 degrees F to preheat.
6. Press "Start/Stop" to begin preheating.
7. In a bowl, add the eggs, sugar and vanilla extract and blend until light and frothy.
8. Slowly, add the chocolate mixture and beat again until well combined.
9. Place the mixture into a lightly greased springform pan.
10. When the display shows "Add Food" open the lid and place the springform pan into the "Crisper Basket".
11. Close the Ninja Air Smart XL Indoor Grill with lid and set the time for 35 minutes.
12. Press "Start/Stop" to begin cooking.
13. When the cooking time is completed, press "Start/Stop" to stop cooking.
14. Open the lid and place the pan onto a wire rack to cool for about 10 minutes.
15. Carefully invert the cake onto the wire rack to cool completely.
16. Cut into desired-sized slices and serve.

Nutritional Information per Serving:

- Calories 247
- Total Fat 20.2 g
- Saturated Fat 12.1 g
- Cholesterol 123 mg
- Sodium 140 mg
- Total Carbs 15.3 g
- Fiber 0 g
- Sugar 13.9 g
- Protein 3.6 g

Cherry Clafoutis

Preparation Time: 15 minutes
Cooking Time: 25 minutes
Servings: 4
Ingredients:

- 1½ cups fresh cherries, pitted
- 3 tablespoons vodka

- ¼ cup flour
- 2 tablespoons sugar
- Pinch of salt
- ½ cup sour cream
- 1 egg
- 1 tablespoon butter
- ¼ cup powdered sugar

Method:

1. In a bowl, mix together the cherries and vodka.
2. In another bowl, place the flour, sugar and salt and mix well.
3. Add the sour cream, and egg and mix until a smooth dough forms.
4. Place the flour mixture into a greased cake pan evenly.
5. Spread cherry mixture over the dough evenly.
6. Now, place the butter on top in the form of dots.
7. Arrange the "Crisper Basket" in the pot of Ninja Air Smart XL Indoor Grill.
8. Close the Ninja Air Smart XL Indoor Grill with lid and select "Air Crisp".
9. Set the temperature to 355 degrees F to preheat.
10. Press "Start/Stop" to begin preheating.
11. When the display shows "Add Food" open the lid and place the cake pan into the "Crisper Basket".
12. Close the Ninja Air Smart XL Indoor Grill with lid and set the time for 25 minutes.
13. Press "Start/Stop" to begin cooking.
14. When the cooking time is completed, press "Start/Stop" to stop cooking.
15. Open the lid and transfer the cake pan onto a wire rack to cool for about 10 minutes.
16. Now, invert the Clafoutis onto a platter and sprinkle with powdered sugar.
17. Cut the Clafoutis into desired-sized slices and serve warm.

Nutritional Information per Serving:

- Calories 241
- Total Fat 10.1 g
- Saturated 5.9 g
- Cholesterol 61 mg
- Sodium 90 mg
- Total Carbs 29 g
- Fiber 1.3 g
- Sugar 20.6 g
- Protein 3.9 g

Conclusion

Did you like all those beefy delights, juicy poultry, and seafood meals? Do you love you to enjoy grilled veggies and fruits? Then stop thinking and bring this smart grill home. This appliance can meet all your Air fryer, oven, and Grill needs. Now you can grill, bake, roast, the air crisp, and even dehydrate a variety of food in one place. No mess, no fuss, and quick results- that's something that every good kitchen need. Once you get your hands on this indoor grill, try the best of the recipes from the cookbook and spread the joy of good flavors.

CPSIA information can be obtained
at www.ICGtesting.com
Printed in the USA
LVHW101128190121
676772LV00023B/246